SO-AGF-543

CULTURE
AS
WEAPON

NATO THOMPSON

CULTURE AS WEAPON

THE ART OF INFLUENCE IN EVERYDAY LIFE

MELVILLE HOUSE
BROOKLYN • LONDON

CULTURE AS WEAPON

First Melville House Printing: January 2017

Melville House Publishing   8 Blackstock Mews
            46 John Street   and   Islington
        Brooklyn, NY 11201   London N4 2BT

mhpbooks.com   facebook.com/mhpbooks   @melvillehouse

ISBN: 978-1-61219-573-5

Design by Jo Anne Metsch

Printed in the United States of America
1   3   5   7   9   10   8   6   4   2

A catalog record for this book is available
from the Library of Congress

CONTENTS

INTRODUCTION

As every artist knows, Plato argued that artists should
be banned from society. A believer that we live in a pale
shadow of a world of perfect forms, he felt that the arts
were dangerous imitations, three degrees removed from
the world of ideal forms. He feared that the arts could stir
the passions of the populace, muddying the objective rationality required in the republic.

Plato's opinion certainly runs counter to the operating
logic of society today. The United States is a consumer society awash in the products of culture. I consider movies,
online programming, video games, advertisements, sports,
retail outlets, music, art museums, and social networking all
a part of the arts, as they all influence our emotions, actions,
and our very understanding of ourselves as citizens. And as
much as politicians would never call themselves artists, they
all understand the value of showmanship and public rela-

tions when it comes to the machinations of governance. But as much as I would like to simply discard Plato's warning, it certainly haunted the writing of this book. For that artistic technique of stirring the passions and appealing to the intimate side in each of us has become inseparable from power.

In *Culture as Weapon*, I do not seek to uncover a cultural conspiracy that puppet masters deploy culture to brainwash us. Instead, I want to explain the ways in which those in power have to use culture to maintain and expand their influence, and the role that we all play in that process. Throughout the twentieth century and into the contemporary era, the world has witnessed the realization of age-old avant-garde demand that art become part of the everyday. Art and life have in fact merged.

At first blush, this train of thought strikes us as fairly obvious. We understand that media is a crucial part of how the world works. We understand that advertising has creeped into many facets of consumer life. And we even understand that spin has come to be a critical part of the political landscape. Ultimately, we understand that message-craft and manipulating the world to cater to how we feel has ingrained itself into every mechanism of power. So, if none of this is new, why write a book?

Simply stated, the industries dependent on shaping how we think have reached an unprecedented scale. As a global strategy deployed at every level, culture has become a profound, and ubiquitous, weapon. Communications and public-relations departments have become essential parts of every business. Global spending on advertising reached nearly $600 billion in 2015.[1] One in seven people on the planet are on Facebook. By 2011, 91 percent of children ages two to seventeen played video games.[2] In the United States, teenagers spend nearly nine hours a day looking at screens.[3] And those are just the measurable aspects of culture's exponential growth. There are countless philosophical questions to be asked: How has the role of music in everyday life changed in the last one hundred years? How many scripted television shows can one watch? How many more creative ways are there to shape the city?

And yet, we remain unappreciative of just how dramatic this shift in the techniques of power has become. In particular, we continue to read the world as though it still has one foot solidly planted in the realm of reason. It is in our global DNA to identify as rational subjects. But perhaps, this Enlightenment-era thinking could use a heavy pause as we discover just how emotional, affective, we truly are.

Certainly this turn away from an Enlightment belief in our own rationality stands on the shoulders of great thinkers from Adorno to Gramsci, from cultural studies of the Birmingham school with figures such as Stuart Hall, Dick Hebidge, and Raymond Williams, to more contemporary, less structuralist, approaches by Judith Butler. But while I invoke some of these theories in the book, my main goal is to make sense of just how affective, how culturally savvy are the institutions—Apple stores, Facebook, real-estate moguls, to name just a few—that we confront daily.

I hope to demonstrate a broad-strokes reading of the

uses of culture. We will define culture simply. And in doing so, we begin to see it everywhere, from counterinsurgency tactics in the Iraq War to the origins of IKEA to rock bands singing for aid for Africa to the design of the Mac to the war on drugs. It is a motley assemblage of seemingly disparate phenomena—and intentionally so. For power is visible in the hands of our elected officials as often as it is hidden in a package of inanity. The many forms of power in our world have sophisticated approaches to reaching that very needy, fearful, and social creature we call ourselves.

One of my key hopes for this book is to echo something that Walter Lippmann had voiced long ago: that democracy is a fallible project rhetorically dependent on a rational subject, who, quite frankly, does not exist. In fact, the illusion of the rational subject has been extremely helpful in hiding the totality of these techniques. Understanding the power of association and the uses of emotion can explain a U.S. election better than a lens of capitalism. Just as Marxist philosophers in Britain sought to understand why the British populace turned away from Labour through the rise of Margaret Thatcher, just as Thomas Frank struggled to understand why working-class Kansas voted Republican, and just as, further back, Karl Marx asked why the French people rallied around the tyrant Louis Bonaparte in 1852, I want to make a further contribution to the cultural study of why people don't act rationally.

While it is certainly demonstrable that one can encourage a consumer to purchase Coca-Cola through a clever, large-scale advertising campaign, it remains unclear how the aggregate of advertising approaches collectively affect the opinions and actions of that consumer. It also remains unclear the secondary results of cultural manipulation when deployed by politicians, whether in the case of war abroad or at home. These cumulative effects of the deployment of affect has made for a very messy social terrain. It is sort of like a greenhouse effect of cultural production that changes our sense of the world around us.

Some compelling implications arise when we read power through its use of culture. For example, power has contributed to the strategies and vulnerabilities of social movements by manipulating media and public perception. Media activism and social movements that cull from the techniques of advertising to make a larger point have a long history, but it is useful to appreciate the double-edged nature of deploying culture. Simple facts—that fear motivates faster than hope, that appeals to emotion do not rely on the truth, or that rationality need not drive enthusiasm—make the terrain of activism that uses culture more precarious.

From an arts perspective, I would like to place what is considered the traditional arts (theater, visual arts, dance, and film) into conversation with not only the commercial arts, but also public relations and advertising. In this way, we can position this more broad definition of art as something that has a potentiality for being both deeply coercive and absolutely powerful. After a century of cultural manipulation, it would be naive to discuss art without simultaneously discussing the manner in which art is already deployed by power daily. With real-estate developers and the tech boom both boldly embracing the power of art to change society, with the deployment of the use of the term *creative* to rebrand innovative capitalist design as an art, one has to appreciate, and perhaps second-guess, just how far art has come. By demystifying the inherent good of art, one can place art in the same conversation as other phenomena of daily life.

As much as this book is about public opinion, I know that public opinion is not everything. In fact, I would say a large part of power doesn't depend on public opinion. The Fortune 500 companies list Walmart at number one with its basic approach of low-cost consumer goods being its strategy. The second company is ExxonMobil, who continues to churn out oil for an energy dependent globe. For both of these companies, power resides in getting the basic goods to people while controlling that market. Yes, they advertise and to some degree shape their brand, but that isn't the formula for their massive sales. So while the uses of culture have grown immensely, they don't exist in a vacuum.

That said, how we understand the world certainly remains a key part of our collective journey. It's an obvious thing to say. But perhaps we have to appreciate that we, as evolutionary creatures, are ultimately fearful social beings who try our best to grapple with phenomena beyond our ken. We try to understand everything from climate change to global war to capitalism to biotechnology. But we can only process that information through the lens of our intimate selves. We interpret the world by way of our personal needs and desires, and so we are vulnerable to larger powers who know how to speak to those needs.

CULTURE
AS
WEAPON

1

THE REAL CULTURE WAR

> There is a religious war going on in our country
> for the soul of America. It is a cultural war, as crit-
> ical to the kind of nation we will one day be as was
> the Cold War itself.
>
> —PATRICK BUCHANAN

Donald Trump's extraordinary ascent in 2015 and 2016
may have undermined much of what we understand about
American politics, but it has also reaffirmed a truth almost
forgotten: as Pat Buchanan goes, so goes the Republican
Party.

When Buchanan spoke at the 1992 Republican convention, his hyperbolic appeals to the human soul echoed a
growing furor in his party. After eight years of Reagan and
four years of Bush, it was no longer enough to define American values. It was time to look inward—to fight the war
within. Buchanan did not get the Republican nomination,
but his diagnosis ("a religious war . . . for the soul of America") would have a tremendous impact in the years to come.

But what, exactly, was that impact? For those American liberals who still remember the culture war—and their number is decreasing—the story is a straightforward one: the fear of change—of cultural irrelevance—was used by Republicans to sustain an increasingly white, increasingly aging coalition. Postmodernity had sunk its teeth into the heart of the United States, and the salt of the earth were scrambling to get their bearings: the parts of the United States that had frowned upon the upheaval of the 1960s could be mobilized into action. Artists would be collateral damage.

In the popular liberal lore, then, the culture war has become synonymous with a cheap form of politics perpetuated by the American right. But the culture wars were more than a battle between darkness and light, between conservatism and liberalism, between the past and the future. Something else was at work.

Everyone who works in the arts has been indoctrinated into the origin story of the culture war. From within, it was a story of contraction and fear. In the span of only a few years in the late 1980s and early '90s, direct grants to artists were eliminated, and the National Endowment for the Arts (NEA) was forced to confront a pattern of budgets cuts that diminished an already impoverished federal department. The arts became a focal point for a party determined to galvanize the masses of white anger against liberalism, democracy, and freedom of expression. The land of Robert Mapplethorpe and Karen Finley, of AIDS activism and socialist leanings, of queer-friendly attitudes and bohemian lifestyles—this land was condemned and stigmatized.

Looking back, though, it's hard not to see a double game at work. If the narrative of evil Republicans and victimized Democrats seems somehow too familiar, too cozy, that's because it is. To see the culture wars as a story of culture—of Culture—as a victim is to miss the methods with which the war was fought. The culture war wasn't a war on culture—at least, not exclusively. It was also a war that *used* culture.

This strategic deployment of culture was both an improvement and an innovation; many of these methods had been developed decades earlier in the field of public relations. Three decades later, we can see examples across the political and social spectrum. Today, culture is a weapon deployed by Democrats and Republicans, by the news media and by powerful corporations, by architects and social-media developers. To an extent that would have been difficult to fathom in the early 1990s, competing uses of culture are no longer a sideshow; they have moved toward the very center of American life.

This is not to suggest, of course, that there exists some glorious, logical past in which our politics were free of irrationality, emotion, or fear. As long as there have been politicians, business leaders, ad executives, activists, artists, hucksters, and public-relations experts, there has been a shared awareness that battles in public life are not fought and won purely on the basis of logic and information. What has changed is scale. Advertising now pervades every aspect of daily life, and public-relations departments—once a novelty—have become critical components of every business and nonprofit.

This is, above all, a book about that investigates the consequences of this shift in scale. It is about the transformative change in the uses of culture by the disparate network of people and institutions we'll call—perhaps a bit hyperbolically—"the powerful."

But it is also a book about artists. Emotion, affect, manipulation—the very tools key to the cultural shift I intend to describe are, after all, tools artists have deployed for centuries. These tools have been captured and coopted, and this, in turn, has had an impact on how artists work. (This is not to say that all artists—or most artists—have stood in opposition to power. Indeed, throughout history, many of them produced little more than a kind of advertising campaign for the powerful—think of court painters or sculptors who ultimately produced fetish objects for the wealthy.)

Which artists are most salient to this discussion of the deployment of culture by the powerful? Whose work and life overlap with the concerns I'm laying out in this book? I'd like to briefly suggest three imperfect categories of artists.

First, there are the oracles: artists that conjure visions of the future through their art. These are artists such as Andy Warhol, who could see, with peculiar clarity, the imminent fusion of consumerism and visual culture.

Second, there are the resisters: artists who use their art to resist the forces of the powerful. This group could include everyone from antiwar poster artists, to artist-activists like Abbie Hoffman (who dumped dollar bills onto the floor of the New York Stock Exchange to demonstrate the inherent greed of American financial capitalism), to artists who practice a more conceptual approach, such as Adrian Piper, whose interventions in New York urban life in the 1970s brought into relief questions of race and gender.

Third, there are the world makers. These are artists who create, through their art, alternative ways of living. Think of Robert Mapplethorpe, the photographer who, in giving an active visual representation of homosexual culture, brought a world into the public light.

This, then, is a story approached from two angles. Throughout this book, I will hone in on groups and individuals who understand that culture is a tool. The goal is not to counterpoise the noble artist against the cynical advertising executive: I am more interested in the evolution and growing complexity of cultural manipulation over the last few decades than I am in condemning that manipulation. Still, I do not want to draw a false equivalence. Art, even at its most public and most ambitious, doesn't have nearly the kind of effect that the culture industries can have. It's also true that the story art can tell is more contingent, more radical, and ultimately far less beholden to power.

We will move back and forth, in historic leaps and bounds, between artists and the groups that deploy culture to their own ends. This approach requires explicating certain industries and histories in detail, even if some of the protagonists—Starbucks, IKEA, the advertising executives paid to market luxury condominiums—seem prosaic and banal. But in that banality lies the truth of culture as it exists today: culture is a dangerous device, culture is a twenty-first-century weapon.

We will first turn to the culture war, a historic moment when the two parts of our story—culture as weapon, launched by the powerful, and culture as a tool, deployed by artists—found themselves facing off in the battlefield of politics.

MORNING IN AMERICA

In 1980, Ronald Reagan's presidential campaign against Jimmy Carter hadn't required much cultural weaponry: skyrocketing oil prices, the hostage crisis in Tehran, and the early spasms of deindustrialization were potent symbols; they didn't need significant elaboration.

But for reelection in 1984, Reagan made a stronger pitch. Some of the largest advertising agencies in the country helped the campaign develop a tone that would stand not only for the candidate, but also for his era. By the time the advertising executive Hal Riney created "Morning in America," the most influential ad of the 1984 campaign, he had been in the advertising industry for decades, including a stint in the military's public-relations office. "Morning in

America" brought to life the nostalgic vision for the future that would help secure Reagan's second term.

The ad begins with images of Americans quietly at work. A fishing boat heads out to sea in the dawn, a businessman exits his taxi, a farmer works his fields, a paperboy delivers the papers, another businessman waves goodbye to his family before getting in his station wagon. Homes are fixed, families are wed. Riney himself delivers the voiceover:

> It's morning again in America. Today, more men and women will go to work than ever before in our country's history. With interest rates at about half the record highs of 1980, nearly 2,000 families today will buy new homes, more than at any time in the past four years. This afternoon, 6,500 young men and women will be married, and with inflation at less than half of what it was just four years ago, they can look forward with confidence to the future. It's morning again in America, and under the leadership of President Reagan, our country is prouder and stronger and better. Why would we ever want to return to where we were less than four short years ago?

The advertisement's strength lies in its subtle shifts from the general to the specific, its leaps between the vague past and the concrete present. In any given sentence, we move from jobs to homes to marriage to inflation to nostalgia, the ad's animating spirit.

Another of the campaign's ads—also produced by

Riney—perhaps best captures the flip side of Reagan's "aw shucks" American optimism. Titled "Bear," the advertisement is an extraordinary document of American Cold War paranoia. As a brown bear wanders through the woods, we hear the following script:

> There is a bear in the woods. For some people, the bear is easy to see. Others don't see it at all. Some people say the bear is tame. Others say it's vicious—and dangerous. Since no one can really be sure who's right, isn't it smart to be as strong as the bear? If there is a bear.

More Zen koan than narrative, this peculiar parable— also read in Hal Riney's sonorous, avuncular voice—hints at the rising power of the Soviet Union and Reagan's capacity to wield a big stick. But it's only that—a hint. Or perhaps a riddle, or a campfire tale: every viewer gets to imagine her own bear, and the campaign trail thus becomes a locus for all manner of private fears.

Riney's two contributions to the Reagan campaign are as apt a metaphor as one can find for America's turn toward nostalgia during the 1980s—a turn that seems particularly striking when one recalls the many visible artistic, cultural, and political movements and subcultures promoting the opposite message during the era. (A partial list might include everything from Run-D.M.C. to the antinuke movement to the aforementioned Mapplethorpe, about whom more in a moment.) But this shift was more than organic; it was, in effect, a weaponized transformation: in only a few short years, what began with advertising would gravitate toward the center of politics.

What Buchanan described as a culture war in his convention speech was both about conservative politicians' specific confrontations with left-wing artists, and simultaneously about a larger clash of values. This war was between a mostly white, mostly Christian community of nostalgists and a sexually open-minded, politically progressive constituency open to cultural change and artistic transformation. The "silent majority" Richard Nixon had first identified in 1969 now had a mouthpiece, while the artists, activists, and radicals who had begun their very public work in the late 1960s were ready to go further, to make their presence known.

"HE IS NOT AN ARTIST, HE IS A JERK."

If Hal Riney was an expert propagandist in what we might call the broader culture war, North Carolina senator Jesse Helms was the brilliant general tasked with ground combat in the more targeted culture war—the assault on the artists.

On May 18, 1989, Helms offered his verdict on the artist Andres Serrano, whose infamous photograph, *Piss Christ*, depicted a crucifix submerged in his own urine. "I do not know Mr. Andres Serrano," Helms said from the Senate floor, "and I hope I never meet him. Because he is not an artist, he is a jerk ... Let him be a jerk on his own time and with his own resources. Do not dishonor our Lord."

Two months later, Helms introduced amendment 420, a controversial bill whose purpose was "To prohibit the use of appropriated funds for the dissemination, promotion, or production of obscene or indecent materials or materials denigrating a particular religion." The target was obvious: the National Endowment of the Arts, which had supported Mapplethorpe's openly homosexual photography ("obscene") and Serrano's provocations ("denigrating a particular religion").

Attacking the NEA, which served the interests of the Republicans' political rivals, was a foolproof political strategy. Ronald Reagan had first attempted to eliminate the NEA in 1980, and by the end of the decade, the wildness and radicalism of artists like Serrano and Mapplethrope presented an irresistible opportunity for confrontation. In June 1989, Rev. Donald Wildmon of the American Family Association (AFA) released a statement condemning Serrano and his *Piss Christ* as blasphemous, and politicians like Helms, Buchanan, New York senator Alfonse D'Amato, and Texas congressman Dick Armey picked up the ball, if they hadn't already.

Yet for most people who followed contemporary art at the time, the idea that an artist might tussle with religion or revel in queer culture didn't seem especially shocking. Indeed, by the time his name received congressional attention, Serrano had been doing this kind of work for nearly a decade. It was edgy, but it was unlikely to freak out gallery goers; if anything, his photographs had a professional, commercial sheen, which would have been impossible to convey to Helms and his supporters.

Serrano grew up in Williamsburg, Brooklyn, the only child of a Honduran father and an Afro-Caribbean mother. He dropped out of high school, but attended art school, where he began to incorporate bodily fluids, dead animals, and religious iconography into his work. As his surrealist photographs began to garner significant attention, Serrano also spent time with a growing counterculture New York art scene. By the time *Piss Christ* gained Jesse Helms's attention, Serrano was something of an insider, and the photograph had been on view—on and off—since 1986, in New York, and in an exhibition organized by the Southeastern Center for Contemporary Art (whose NEA grant was the source of all the controversy that followed).[4]

That Serrano was from New York and emerged from its bohemian subcultures was far from incidental. In fact, New York was key to the success and controversies of many of the artists implicated in the culture war. Mapplethorpe was perhaps the paradigmatic example of an artist who remained committed to the battles and freedoms won and fought for in the 1960s and 1970s: like Serrano, he made visible that which many hoped would simply disappear, and New York was where this visibility could assert itself. A photographer since the 1960s, Mapplethorpe was an unapologetic, enthusiastic participant in the homoerotic subculture of the New York City he was born in. For the photographer, the camera was merely part of an overall sexual experience. "For me," Mapplethorpe said, "S&M means sex and magic, not sadomasochism."[5]

The focus of the attack on Mapplethorpe was the traveling retrospective *Robert Mapplethorpe: The Perfect Moment*, organized by the Philadelphia Institute of Contemporary Art (ICA) and curator Janet Kardon. Two weeks before its opening at the Corcoran Gallery of Art in Washington, D.C., Donald Wildmon's American Family Association brought its campaign against "indecent" art to the attention of the Corcoran board. The Corcoran canceled the show.

The fight over the Mapplethorpe retrospective was even more dramatic than the one over *Piss Christ*. It took a lot of work to be more offensive than Jesus dumped in piss, but if someone could do it, it was the naughty, leather-bound visionary. Mapplethorpe's iconic black-and-white photographs explored not only homosexuality, but homosexual sexuality, which made for a particularly vivid controversy: by attacking the NEA, politicians could gay bash on cable television. In one self-portrait, Mapplethorpe turns back to the camera in chaps and holds a whip that extrudes from his ass: a perfect image to sear into the collective unconscious of a constituency terrified by gay people and gay rights.

Naturally, there were other controversies. Also in 1989, Dread Scott Tyler, a twenty-four-year-old artist and art student, came under fire for *What is the Proper Way to Display the U.S. Flag?* on view at the School of the Art Institute of Chicago. The piece featured a photomontage of flag burn-

ings and flags draped over coffins. Below the image lay a
blank book for visitors to contribute their own thoughts on
the subject, and below that was an actual American flag,
which one would need to stand on in order to write in the
book. To participate in the artwork, visitors had to des-
ecrate the flag.

The response was predictable. Veterans were outraged,
and President George Bush, Sr., called the artwork "dis-
graceful." One offended art teacher even painted a police
outline of Tyler, upon which people could walk in order to
look at an American flag respectfully hung on the wall. A
1989 article from *The New York Times* captures the spirit of
the response:

> Call it performance art, Chicago-style. About 3,000
> protesters, many of them veterans, flocked to the steps
> of the Art Institute of Chicago on Sunday to protest an
> exhibit that, they charge, desecrates the American flag.
> Some did it by desecrating the Soviet flag. Others car-
> ried patriotic signs and flags as they sang and chanted.
> Some railed against the "satanic communists" they held
> responsible for the "travesty" inside.

The show had to be temporarily cancelled—not once,
but twice—and the Chicago City Council unanimously
passed an ordinance enforcing six months in jail and a $250
fine for anyone found mutilating or defacing the flag. And
in a triumph of bipartisanship, Republican senator Bob
Dole and Democratic senator Alan Dixon cosponsored a

flag desecration bill that passed unanimously. Meanwhile, the participatory comments book in Dread Scott's artwork became a sort of Rorschach test for the American mood at that time. A sampling of the messages:[6]

> Go fuck yourself Dread Scott Tyler. You are lucky to be living in this country. See you in hell. —Chicago Police Officer

> I think it's ridiculous that our entire country is symbolized in a flag, an idiotic piece of cloth. It's time people start questioning a country that says it supports freedoms of all sorts when one can't even step on a piece of cloth.

> Dear Dread, It is a disgrace to display America like this. Who do you think you are? A small time minority looking for attention—you asshole! If you don't love this country leave it. FUCK YOU.

Given our familiarity with clickbait and slanderous internet comments and the perpetual whirring of the outrage machine, we can appreciate the drama over Serrano, Mapplethorpe, and Tyler as more of the same, only in embryonic form. This appreciation would be entirely accurate as long as we understand just how pervasive these techniques have since become. The cultural battles taking place in the late 1980s seem, in retrospect, like the ascent of something new then and ubiquitous now. Here were news stories driven and dominated by shock and indignation—stories that could essentially be reenacted and regurgitated by the media with little concern for judgment or conclusions. The various battles of the culture war were surely not the first instance of collective moral panic reinforced by the news media, but it's hard not to see the interchangeability of news and outrage as a prefiguration of our cultural condition. In other words, it's not just angry comments, it's a perfect fusion of culture and politics.

A year after Serrano, Mapplethorpe, and Tyler, Americans learned the name John Frohnmayer. Frohnmayer wasn't another controversial artist; he was, rather, the unassuming fifth chairman of the NEA, appointed by George H. W. Bush in 1989. Unassuming, that is, until 1990. On June 29, Frohnmayer vetoed program grants to artists Karen Finley, John Fleck, Holly Hughes, and Tim Miller, who subsequently became known as the NEA Four.

Unsurprisingly, in their rejected performances, the four artists explored sexuality and the concerns of oppressed communities (especially queer, lesbian, and female communities). Hughes's were called *The Well of Horniness* and *The Lady Dick*, which should speak to the objections. Finley, in a piece called *We Keep Our Victims Ready*, covered her naked body in chocolate, "a symbol of women being treated like dirt."[7] Fleck's *Blessed Are the Little Fishes* actively explored the artist's homosexuality and Catholic upbringing—and featured a toilet, which couldn't have pleased the authorities. Miller, meanwhile, made even the language of his grant provocative, writing that he "told Jesse Helms to keep his Porky Pig face out of the NEA and out of my asshole."[8]

Speaking to the NEA panel, Frohnmayer put it aptly: "We are in a no-win situation folks."[9]

Naturally, the veto produced a vast backlash and catapulted the artists into the limelight. In a letter to the editor of *The Washington Post*, Finley wrote, "I know that a witch-hunt of the arts does not truly represent the wishes of the American people but merely those of a fanatic faction. Americans want controversial artists to be funded, and the evidence is there in a new nationwide poll. I hope American citizens of different backgrounds will be able to continue to express themselves freely without fear of censorship."[10]

It didn't quite work out that way.

Which isn't to say that artists had no defenders in Congress. Certainly, there were outliers: during an appropriations meeting in 1990, New York representative Edolphus Towns said, "In essence, art allows us to overcome, transcend, and be made sublime. Those who oppose art oppose openness, and new ideas. To oppose art is to oppose the potential inherent in each of us. To oppose art is to oppose yourself."[11] But for most congressmen and congresswomen—especially those not from Brooklyn—the NEA hubbub was an opportunity to condemn luridness and bask in it in equal measure.

The Republican Party had learned that one could gain the public's attention by sensationalizing a behavior or an artistic practice and criticize it at the same time. Pornography, homosexual sex, feminist liberation, anti-

Americanism—all of this was wrong and produced anxiety in a fearful public, and yet it was hard to resist this alluring material: one could stand back and decry it while making it the center of attention. And if politicians and their constituents were eager to yell and gawk, the news media was thrilled to fan the flames. In their desperate effort to stop the spread of deviance across America, the Republicans turned to the airwaves, the newspapers, and the magazines. Writing about sexuality in the nineteenth century, Michel Foucault might well have been describing the American cultural landscape circa 1990:

> Rather than the uniform concern to hide sex, rather than a general prudishness of language, what distinguishes these last three centuries is the variety, the wide dispersion of devices that were invented for speaking about it, for having it be spoken about, for inducing it to speak of itself, for listening, recording, transcribing, and redistributing what is said about it: around sex, a whole network of varying, specific, and coercive transpositions into discourse. Rather than a massive censorship, beginning with the verbal proprieties imposed by the Age of Reason, what was involved was a regulated and polymorphous incitement to discourse.

It is a pattern with which we have become familiar.

DOGGEREL AS SERMON

> People will fall over cut glass to get what you tell
> them they can't have.
>
> —BRUCE ROGOW, the lead lawyer
> for 2 Live Crew, 1990[12]

The visual arts were just one front in the culture war. Just as elitist, state-funded art was supposedly corrupting our society, mainstream, unabashedly capitalist music was supposedly hurting our children. Fortunately, Tipper Gore was on the case.

In 1985, Gore heard her daughter listening to the Prince's gloriously perverse, deliciously nasty "Darling Nikki." Prince was at the peak of his fame, and between *Purple Rain* (the album) and *Purple Rain* (the movie), he was inescapable. Which was why children like Gore's eleven-year-old daughter Karenna were listening to a song about a nymphomaniac with the following lyrics: "I knew a girl named Nikki / I guess you could say she was a sex fiend."

Thus the Parents Resource Music Center (PRMC) was born. The PRMC proposed adding warning labels on albums considered to possess adult content and compiled a list of fifteen songs they felt epitomized their concerns, widely known as the Filthy Fifteen. Not unlike the circus that erupted during the Mapplethorpe scandal, the PRMC's proposals provoked a national uproar. A Senate hearing was held, and a diverse group of musicians went to Congress to pay tribute to freedom of expression. Twisted Sister's Dee Snider, folk musician John Denver, and art rock superstar Frank Zappa all made rather ham-fisted declarations about democracy in a pro-toreality television spectacle that relied on celebrity for its appeal.

The PRMC's Susan Baker (wife of the secretary of the treasury) argued: "There certainly are many causes for these ills in our society, but it is our contention that the pervasive messages aimed at children which promote and glorify suicide, rape, sadomasochism, and so on, have to be numbered among the contributing factors." Here, again, was an expression of anxiety about American values— about the unfamiliar world the United States' children were encountering.

But most of all, the entire confrontation made for great television. How could any TV viewer resist tuning in as Snyder explained to Gore that, yes, while his band's fan club was called "Sick Mother Fucking Fans of Twisted Sister," he was nonetheless a good Christian?

For its part, the PRMC succeeded in instituting its warning labels, which, as one might guess, only helped sales. And a couple of years later, Donald Wildmon's American Family Association took a page from the PRMC playbook and turned their attention from audio to textual obscenity. Setting their sights on 2 Live Crew, Miami's most outrageous booty bass ensemble, the AFA decided that warning labels were not enough where songs like "Me So Horny" were concerned.

The lyrics to "Me So Horny" were raw and dirty. ("I

know he'll be disgusted when he sees your pussy busted / Won't your mama be so mad if she knew I got that ass?" is just a modest sample.) They objectified women and they offended common decency. But so, too, did a lot of music. Like the NEA scandal, the war between the AFA and 2 Live Crew was ultimately less about specific lyrics than about a media spectacle that combined vulgarity and condemnation. In June 1989, U.S. District Court judge Jose Gonzales declared 2 Live Crew's album obscene. Not long after, a record store owner found himself on television, in handcuffs, for selling the illicit album to an undercover agent. And after that, Luther Campbell and 2 Live Crew were arrested for performing their album in concert. For everyone but the people directly implicated, it was a win-win: you could enjoy the scolding and the object of that scolding all at once.

Patrick Buchanan failed to win the Republican nomination in 1992, and that same year, George H. W. Bush asked Frohnmayer to resign, a week after Buchanan accused the Bush administration of "subsidizing both filthy and blasphemous art." The fight over subsidized art and censorship would recede from its intense highs, but even as one culture war was coming to a close, the other, larger culture war was gaining strength. Wasn't Fleetwood Mac's "Don't Stop Thinking About Tomorrow"—Bill Clinton's campaign song—not much more than an ideologically and aesthetically palatable version of "Morning in America"? Indeed, the Clinton campaign deployed culture far more aggressively than any previous politician: here, after all, was the

Democratic nominee on MTV and on Arsenio Hall, playing the saxophone while angling for the youth vote.
Culture was no longer the enemy. It was the weapon.

DOUBLE GAME

As we've seen, the culture war was influential in part because its lessons are more ambiguous than they first appear.
What took place in the late 1980s and early '90s wasn't
merely a war between two cultures, but a broader realign-
ment. A number of forces were learning to utilize the power
of culture to push forward their own agendas, and their successes would be grander and more pronounced than before.

During the culture war, artists were certainly victimized—as were some of the institutions that supported them.
(In the NEA's case, the damage was especially severe.). Yet
at least for a time, some of those same artists also attained
a fame wildly incommensurate with what they might have
dreamt of at the beginning of their careers. One could argue that their fame—that onslaught of visibility—was itself
a kind of turning point. Visual artists had successfully lev-
eraged the media in the past, of course (think of Salvador
Dali appearing on late-night television), but in its scale and
saturation, this media attention was something new.

To put it simply, the more culture we take in, the more
we as consumers become aware and accustomed to it. Generations have now grown up under a historically unique

level of cultural bombardment. A few numbers can make the point. In 1950, 9 percent of American homes had televisions; by 1959, that number had grown to 85.9 percent; and by 1978, it was at 98 percent.[13]

My emphasis on scale and saturation suggests that this cultural turn wasn't bound to a particular ideology or to a rigidly defined set of heroes and villains. Or, for that matter, to a fixed understanding of intention and causality. A media executive, politician, or a cultural figure's culpability for a specific form of cultural manipulation—or a media executive's *passionate belief* in his or her goals—is less relevant than the effect of that manipulation. Culture is a vast dynamic imposing itself on everything from politics to media to advertising to warfare.

This dynamic didn't emerge from nowhere: its techniques have been gradually distributed. In the next chapter, we will encounter some of this story's progenitors, including Bill Ivey, Edward Bernays, Leo Burnett, and David Ogilvy. It is hard to believe that in the early twentieth century, businesses did not rely on marketing departments, and politics hadn't yet turned into a battle between rival pollsters, focus-group organizers, and brand strategists.

These techniques understand and utilize emotion, violence, outrage, and fear. Those people and organizations who use culture toward their own ends know that the rational is no match for the affective. And we are thus quite vulnerable to the tools deployed by the most powerful forces in society.

2

THE PERSUADERS

John D. Rockefeller felt misunderstood as he looked over the newspapers spread out on his desk. The headlines read as a coordinated assault on his very personhood: he had become a monster, seemingly overnight. Only recently, he had been the savior of the American economy; now he was the villainous enemy of the American dream. His father had endured his own share of problems at Standard Oil, but now in the twentieth century, a new company had new enemies. Namely, the media, which had, with the proliferation of magazines and newspapers, become much more venomous.

The year was 1914, and a dozen people had died in an attack on striking coal miners in Ludlow, Colorado. The media had eaten it up—they were calling it the Ludlow Massacre—but Rockefeller knew it wasn't his fault. The papers didn't understand that economic growth always had negative consequences: it was a statistical fact that people died unnecessarily, and there was nothing he could do.

Rockefeller needed a new story—a more truthful story: one with different protagonists and different villains. As he saw it, the fault for the deaths lay with the overzealous miners' unions, who had exacerbated the situation. The unions were trying to stoke the public's sympathy to misrepresent what had clearly been an accident—an accident for which they had lain the groundwork.

Rockefeller called Ivy Lee, a young employee of the Pennsylvania Railroad, who was working in the then-emerging field of public relations. Lee advised a strategy that impressed the billionaire. "This is the first advice I have had that does not involve deviousness of one kind or one another," Rockefeller told Lee. "The obviousness of the course you suggest *does* appeal."[14]

What Lee advised was a strategy of transparency. Rather than paying off reporters or posting full-page advertisements that amounted to little more than propaganda, Lee wanted the facts to win the day. Let the coal-mine operators and the National Guard tell their stories. Show that *your* eagerness to get the truth out to the public exceeds that of the reporters on the story, who, after all, may have an agenda. Let the Colorado Fuel and Iron Company win back the hearts of the American public.

And so began Ivy Lee's first great public-relations campaign. Lee released bulletins to shapers of public opinion, including the press, which produced a deluge of facts on the situation in Colorado. His facts, his information. He denied the strike's legitimacy and placed the blame for the lack of law and order squarely on the shoulders of the strike leaders themselves. He demonstrated Rockefeller's limited role in the company, while also showing how much coal mining contributed to the American economy. He demonstrated a mutual interest in fair wages, thus taking the wind out of the strikers' sails. And he made the press realize that Rockefeller had nothing to hide.

Upton Sinclair would later refer to Lee as "Poison Ivy," and historian Howard Zinn would describe the Ludlow Massacre as "the culminating act of perhaps the most violent struggle between corporate power and laboring men in American history."[15] But these descriptions hardly undercut the significance of Lee's accomplishments. Lee understood, before many others, that transparency was complicated— that objectivity was, in itself, just another perspective. So when he advised Rockefeller to tell the truth, he knew that truth wasn't a fixed quantity.

Public opinion, publicity, and public relations all came to prominence toward the end of the nineteenth century, and from there, they only grew in importance. The increased deployment of these industries suggests that over time, power has increasingly come to understand and utilize the tools of culture to sell, manipulate, and excite.

Essential to the rise of techniques designed to cajole, provoke, placate, and outrage is a shared understanding of human fallibility. Every successful PR executive and every advertiser has understood that people can be reduced to their emotions, which can then be manipulated.

Though the following two chapters will discuss the increased professionalization and sophistication of public relations and advertising, their true subject is the emergence of a set of skills that takes for granted people's fundamental irrationality.

And through the story of that emergence, we'll better understand the ways in which culture is deployed today. The innovations of Ivy Lee will help us grasp the innovations of Karl Rove. The techniques of George Gallup and his focus group will shed light on the interior design that makes the Apple Store so distinctive—and seductive. I hope, too, that a richer understanding of these connections will help us recognize, with greater specificity, the way power operates.

MOBILIZATION

War often provides a major catalyst for innovations in techniques of cultural manipulation, and World War I was no exception.

President Woodrow Wilson had come into office on a platform of nonintervention, but by April 1917, he had declared war on Germany. He understood that in this moment of historic national divisions, he would have to rally the troops and civilians in support of the war effort. The Committee on Public Information (CPI) was the answer.

George Creel was chosen to head up the agency. An

investigative journalist who had emerged from difficult circumstances in Missouri, Creel understood how propaganda could be used to mobilize public opinion. "People do not live by bread alone," he said. "They live mostly by catch phrases."[16] The zeal and energy with which Creel undertook his effort to build support for the war effort proved the truth of his remark.

As usual with propaganda, there was a stick along with the carrot: the Espionage Act, passed in 1917. "Such creatures of passion, disloyalty, and anarchy must be crushed out," Wilson said in 1915. "They are not many, but they are infinitely malignant, and the hand of our power should close over them at once. They have formed plots to destroy property, they have entered into conspiracies against the neutrality of the Government."[17]

Here we see a strategic use of propaganda to redefine the heroes and villains, enacted by Lee previously, being used at a federal level. Over the following years, the CPI and the Espionage Act galvanized national enthusiasm for the war—and suspicion of all its detractors. Though the CPI is long gone—dispersed into more numerous and more sophisticated institutions—the Espionage Act has remained a formidable law for a century, targeting everyone from Julius and Ethel Rosenberg to Daniel Ellsberg to Chelsea Manning.

Creel's greatest success might not have been any individual aspect of the CPI's propaganda, but his skill at avoiding the term entirely. "We did not call it propaganda," he said, "for that word, in German hands, had come to be associated with deceit and corruption."[18] His job, he insisted, was simply communications.

Still, there were many triumphs—think of J. M. Flagg's poster of Uncle Sam pointing a finger and saying, "I Want You for U.S. Army," or Creel's spectacular deployment of the "four-minute men." These nearly 75,000 volunteers demonstrated their oratorical skills and personal passion for the war effort at social events, public gatherings, and in small groups of friends. Why "four-minute" men? At the time, public-opinion experts believed that the average person had an attention span of four minutes. (Today's advertisers surely couldn't imagine what they would do with four whole minutes of people's time.)

Creel's efforts had their detractors, of course. Walter Lippmann, the Pulitzer Prize–winning journalist and *New Republic* founder, viewed Creel as both incompetent and arrogant. Censorship, Lippmann wrote, "should never be entrusted to anyone who is not himself tolerant, not to anyone who is unacquainted with the long record of folly which is the history of suppression."[19]

What Lippmann saw in Creel's efforts echoed his broader concerns about democracy. Like the master propagandist himself, Lippmann believed that the public operated predominantly through what he called "pictures in their heads" and cared little for the actual facts of any particular issue. Consequently, he distrusted power that was concentrated too strongly in one place, believing that power of this kind could manipulate a broad public. The people were too easily misled and the powerful too easily corrupted.

Lippmann's answer to this paradox of democracy laid in the field of journalism itself. Journalism, he felt, should not only communicate the facts, but act as a mediator between an easily befuddled public and an easily corruptible government. In 1922, Lippmann published *Public Opinion*, which offered great insights into the emerging fields of advertising, marketing, and public relations. It also offered—perhaps implicitly—a stark rejection of a fundamental element of democracy: that a voting population could be objective. As Stuart Ewen writes of the period in *PR! A Social History of Spin*, "In the citadels of the Enlightened West, a naïve faith in reason was beginning to fade from view. Publicists were beginning to look for unconscious or instinctive triggers that might be pulled to activate public passions."[20] How, then, could people vote when they clearly didn't know what was really in their interest?

DADA

A focus on wartime propaganda can't ignore the exponentially larger, exponentially more horrific reality of the war itself. World War I was unprecedented in its destruction, and such a human tragedy was bound to have tremendous cultural consequences, especially when counterpoised by the onslaught of prowar iconography and rhetoric that blanketed every participating nation.

The efforts of Creel and the CPI were echoed by—

among others—the propaganda machine in Germany, which tapped into the mythology of Nordic traditions through depictions of dragons, Valkyries, and Wagnerian epoch imagery; the goal, as the propagandists saw it, was to summon latent cultural mythologies in support of present-tense warfare. World War I thus marked the moment when Europe first confronted the overwhelming power of nation-based propaganda.

Against this backdrop of government-sponsored, prowar art, Dada came into being. Dada emerged in 1916 out of a radical nightclub called Cabaret Voltaire. Named after the French philosopher who implored his countrymen to cultivate their own garden as an exercise in self-liberation, the Cabaret Voltaire was an exercise in creative, collective cultural exploration. Poetry readings, sing-alongs, paintings, and plays all coexisted in a smoky, drunken haze occupied by artists and political refugees. Formed by Hugo Ball, Emmy Hennings, and—soon thereafter—Marcel Janco, Richard Huelsenbeck, Tristan Tzara, Sophie Taeuber-Arp, and Jean Arp, the nightclub quickly grew into an artistic enclave that captured a growing disillusionment.

Drawn together in despair, hostility, and a desire for creative freedom, these artists were mortified by the war's destruction, brutality, and utter stupidity. They were disgusted with the war machine, but just as much, they found themselves abandoning the idea of a rational society altogether. If this war were the natural outcome of modernity, they wanted nothing to do with any of it. As Ball wrote in his Dada Manifesto of 1916, "I don't want words that other people have invented. All the words are other people's inventions. I want my own stuff, my own rhythm, and vowels and consonants too, matching the rhythm and all my own."

If Walter Lippmann wanted journalists to interpret the facts for people, Dada wanted people to accept nothing at all from above. Propaganda had to be battled, and because images were being used to conscript, to enlist, and to garner support, they had to be resisted. Thus the name: Dada. The word sounds infantile, antilingual—a baby's first blubbering words. But better to traffic in non-sense than a corrupted kind of sense. The Dadaists wanted their own language— one that wasn't implicated in blood and violence.

Their movement soon spread throughout Europe and across the Atlantic to New York; it seemed that the notion that official images should be resisted at all costs held a growing appeal. Dada showed that disgust was an attractive option in the face of a common political enemy. Take the artist George Grosz, a World War I veteran whose visceral sense of the war's absurdity led him to form the *Neue Sachlichkeit* (New Objectivity) movement with Max Beckmann and Otto Dix. These artists opposed the cascade of materialism and nationalism that defined the Weimar Republic.

In his drawing of Berlin's most famous commercial street, Friedrichstraße, Grosz depicts the denizens of the city under a looming mass of what can only be described as corporate logos. This piece was something new: a recognition that propaganda hadn't ended along with the war effort, but that it had blossomed into something more diffuse and more insidious. Like Lippmann, Grosz understood that even in peacetime, images of power were shaping the minds and emotions of the people. This insight was a remarkable prescience, and we should keep it in mind as we explore a twentieth century defined by just this kind of cultural barrage.

REACH FOR A LUCKY INSTEAD OF A TREAT

A few years later, in 1929, New York's Easter Sunday parade played host to a spectacular display, revealing and lurid (by the period's standards), and in many ways the tonal opposite of Grosz's dark, urban vision. In the middle of the parade was a group of women, proudly lighting up Lucky Strike cigarettes in direct defiance of the public taboo on women smoking in public.

The event was widely reported in the press as an actual protest. "Group of Girls Puff at Cigarettes as a Gesture of 'Freedom,'" read *The New York Times* headline,[21] and according to the *United Press*, "Miss Bertha Hunt and six colleagues [had] struck another blow in behalf of the liberty of women."[22] The event captured the imagination as it redefined gender and smoking all in one go. No one suspected that these reactions had been entirely orchestrated.

Yet a crucial aspect of the performance went unreported: public-relations guru Edward L. Bernays staged the whole thing. Bernays had paid each of the women for their participation on behalf of his client, American Tobacco Company. This classic stunt—neither Bernays's first nor his last—helped define the field of public relations over the following century.

Born in Vienna in 1891, Bernays was boastful, obsessively competitive, and terrifyingly resourceful. (That his aunt was Martha Bernays, Sigmund Freud's wife, is a suggestive piece of family history.) He understood that public relations was about more than clever catchphrases or advertisements—it was, above all, the production of reality. But unlike Ivy Lee, he saw PR as a kind of magic rather than a version of journalism. Bernays understood that PR could produce a mood and a spirit—that facts were necessarily secondary to emotion.

Bernays had been involved—peripherally—with the CPI's efforts, but through his work for American Tobacco he emerged as an innovative force. He knew that existing attitudes were important to his work: he wrote that "institutions which modify public opinion carry on against a background which is also in itself a controlling factor."[23] And so he honed in on that background.

As Bernays saw it, the two issues central to women in the 1920s were body image and freedom. What became known as the Torches of Freedom campaign took care of the latter, and to tackle the former, he came up with a new method: he paid health experts to testify to cigarettes' effectiveness as an appetite suppressor. This testimony seems overheated now—Bernays convinced Arthur Murray, a dancing school owner, to testify that, "Dancers today, when tempted to overindulge at the punch bowl or the buffet, reach for a cigarette instead"—but it was strikingly successful.[24]

"If you can influence the leaders, either with or without their conscious cooperation," Bernays wrote, "you automatically influence the group which they sway."[25] The effect of third-party testimony remains so powerful that it's hard to think of an aspect of contemporary life that hasn't to some extent been affected by the method. Indeed, the leap from cigarettes as weight loss device to climate scientists' well-subsidized skepticism toward climate change is not all that dramatic.

The smoking campaign was one of hundreds. And the clients weren't all corporate: in an attempt to transform President Calvin Coolidge into a warmer, more personable politician, Bernays orchestrated a pancake breakfast attended by celebrities, captured by the news media. Here was the president as human being, and here, too, was the first great modern political publicity stunt. No politician who has visited a state fair in Iowa or a diner in New Hampshire is wholly free from Bernays's influence.

Bernays's client list ranged from Proctor and Gamble to the NAACP to the Aluminum Company of America. And like any consultant, he adapted and refined his skills according to his clients' needs. As the twentieth century progressed, his approach would become a lingua franca. No matter the ideology at work, public relations became inescapable. Bernays's methods are key to the strategies we'll encounter throughout this book.

THE WATER'S TEMPERATURE

If Bernays and Lippmann were the early masters of manufacturing consent, George Gallup was the first to take the
collective temperature. Born to a family of dairy farmers in 1901, Gallup studied journalism at the University
of Iowa. As the editor of the school newspaper, the *Daily
Iowan*, he promoted an unshaking faith in the democratic
project. "Don't be afraid to be radical," he wrote "We need
atheists, free-lovers, anarchists, free traders, communists,
single taxers, internationalists, royalists, socialists, anti-
Christians . . . Doubt everything. Question everything."[26]
His belief in democracy went hand in hand with his early
interest in polling, which initially manifested itself in an
unconventional way: the story goes that Gallup created a
newspaper poll that sought to determine the prettiest girl
on campus; his future wife, Ophelia Miller, won the contest, and they were married in 1925.

As a junior in college, Gallup took a summer job with
D'Arcy Advertising Co. in St. Louis, which would go on
to produce the Santa Claus icon for Coca-Cola and Bud-
weiser's famous catchphrase "This Bud's for You." D'Arcy
was surveying the public to find out what news articles they
read, and Gallup thought the results were unconvincing: "I
found that a high percentage of respondents claimed that
they always read the editorials, the national and international news. Few admitted reading the gossip columns and
other features of low prestige."[27]

This insight shaped his academic interests, and in place

of a Ph.D. thesis, he submitted a new polling method. Titled "An Objective Method for Determining Reader Interest in the Content of a Newspaper," the survey sought to
determine, with greater accuracy, what readers were actually paying attention to. Gallup worked with the local paper, the *Iowa Register*, and discovered that the *Register*'s heady
international-affairs headlines weren't making an impression on readers: the language was too fluffy, and it didn't
move quickly enough. But while "the most important articles published in the newspapers attracted far fewer readers than shown by the typical questionnaire procedure,"
Gallup wrote, "the comic strips, the love advice features
and the like had considerably more readers."[28]

In 1932, Gallup was recruited by the advertising pow-
erhouse Young and Rubicam to head up their emerging
research division. At Young and Rubicam, he studied the
effectiveness of print-media advertising and oversaw the
first-ever research into the impact of radio. But more crucially, that same year, he began his work on election results.
He started with his mother-in-law Ola Babcock Miller's
political campaign, and when she won—becoming the
state's first female secretary of state—Gallup's scientific
poll was widely hailed as the first to predict an election.

Bolstered by his success, Gallup went on to found the
American Institute of Public Opinion in 1935, and in 1936,
he correctly predicted President Roosevelt's win over Republican contender Alf Landon. Gallup was catapulted into
the limelight: if he could predict elections, what else could
he do? How might these public-opinion-monitoring tools

apply to a growing set of industries interested in tailoring their message and products to an equally growing audience?

In the years to come, Gallup would move seamlessly between politics, advertising, journalism, and entertainment, as public relations and polling matured into tools that could, perhaps, shed light on the way power in American life was wielded and manifested itself. Meanwhile, industries across the American landscape showed an increasing interest in—depending on one's degree of sympathy—either cultural manipulation or the tailoring of their products to specific audiences.

OF COPY AND CREATIVES

If the early twentieth century gave birth to public relations and the institutionalization of polling, the field of advertising took these skills as essential in its meteoric rise.

The consumer society had emerged: clothes that fit off the rack were suddenly available, automobiles were conquering city streets, and Americans were learning to live on more than just the essentials. As consumption became an increasing priority, differentiation and perception of new and existing products was often more important than product development itself. By the 1920s, advertising agencies like J. Walter Thompson (clients: Proctor and Gamble, General Electric) and BBDO (Dunlop, General Motors) had become essential parts of corporate life; without their services, companies could not expect to launch successful products. According to Mansel Blackford and K. Austin Kerr in their book, *Business Enterprise in American History*, "In 1919 advertising costs were 8 percent of total distribution costs in industry; by 1929, the share was 14 percent. In that latter year, advertising costs reached nearly $3 billion."[29]

The J. Walter Thompson agency's Stanley Resor and his revolutionary copywriter—and eventual wife—Helen Lansdowne were two of the most influential figures in the advertising revolution. Lansdowne, the first woman to occupy an upper-level position in an ad agency, would have a tremendous influence on a mode that was usually geared toward the woman consumer. "In advertising these products," wrote Lansdowne, "I supplied the feminine point of view."[30] For example, she notably introduced sexual themes into advertising campaigns, such as an ad for soap that read, "A Skin You Love to Touch." Resor, meanwhile, applied his interest in statistics and psychology to a field that, until recently, had been defined more by intuition than analytical rigor. He believed fervently in the science of advertising. With that conviction, he hired economists and psychologists, and like Bernays, Resor widely used third-party testimonials, hiring society doyennes and celebrities to vouch for beauty products. Resor and Lansdowne made J. Walter Thompson that largest ad company of the period.

The venues for advertising were also growing in scale and reach. In 1923, the twenty-five-year-old Henry Robinson Luce and his roommate Briton Hadden started *Time*, the nation's first weekly magazine. With its enormous growth came the potential for advertisers to reach the entire country at once. As Stephen Fox writes in *Mirror Makers*, his remarkable book on the history of advertising, "Advertising would never again have it so plush: the public so uncritically accepting, the economy so robust, the government so approving; the trade at its zenith, high tide and green grass."

New physical spaces for advertising appeared as well. Department and chain stores like Sears, Roebuck, Woolworths, and Walgreen Drug were key to the emergence of consumer culture, and they offered—in addition to a previously unimaginable supply of consumer goods—advertisements in three-dimensional space. Interior designs and window displays became an object of collective fascination, as stores invested greater effort and energy into luring customers inside.

The early days of the consumer culture marked an unprecedented fusion of aesthetics and industry, and naturally, the arts were not impervious to the influences of advertising—and vice versa. The prevailing art movements of the time reveled in wealth, glitz, and glamour. Art Deco, which had been the rage in France before washing up on American shores, borrowed from every artistic style and blended them all with a certain consumerist glee. Here were the angular outbursts of cubism, the speed-driven boldness of futurism, and even the mystical exoticism provoked by the numerous archeological discoveries then under way around the world.

Unlike Deco, the art-in-industry movement had a narrower set of influences: particularly, the British Arts and

Crafts movement. (William Morris, the fervent anticapitalist designer who favored small shops and guilds, would have been shocked and horrified by the appropriation.) Also unlike Deco, art-in-industry was less an artistic movement than a philosophy of retailing: store designers on the cutting edge were deploying high design toward utilitarian ends. In that sense, it was the ultimate symbol of a trend that had become undeniable: a fusion of culture and marketing that used the terms and language of the former to produce the results sought by the latter.

THE SOUND THAT MADE A CRAZE

Radio was different. Radio really was radical—a new technology that quickly transformed not only the way Americans encountered all kinds of culture, but also increased the scale on which that culture could be used to disseminate commercial messages.

Radio was the next great mass medium after newspapers, and indeed, it may have really been the first—the number of people reached by radio far exceeded the circulation figures of even the most successful newspapers of the time: by 1933, two-thirds of American households would own at least one radio.[31]

Like the public-relations industry, the radio emerged as a force during World War I, and it exploded in the following years. Radio gave birth to an extraordinary diversity of capitalist cultural forms to come: everything from programming sponsorships to soap operas, not to mention major communications networks, like ABC and CBS. Even during the Great Depression, with millions in poverty, most Americans felt compelled to own a radio. They had to: not to own a radio was to be detached from what was happening everywhere. The ears of a nation became synchronized and attuned.

Recorded music, too, was in an age of unprecedented ascendance. In the 1890s, records were predominantly consumed in "phonograph parlors": these public areas were far more accessible than expensive concert halls, and were—definitionally—more for average Joes than for connoisseurs. Sheet music remained wildly popular until the 1920s, at which point the sales of records began to skyrocket. Four million records were sold in 1900; nine years later, that number was thirty million; and by 1920, the number had jumped again, dramatically, to 100 million records a year. The extraordinary growth of radio only amplified this effect, and the combined scale of radio and the record industry meant that there was now a national audience for art that might, in the past, have remained small and regional. Jazz was the paradigmatic example of an art that flourished in the radio age.

Jazz emerged out of a combination of African rhythms, Afro-Cuban music, and the classically trained music of ragtime composer Scott Joplin. It was the sound of America's most brutalized and impoverished class, it spoke a language of resistance and freedom, it embodied a generational break (kids loved it, parents hated it), and it marked a critical divide: most music experts argued that jazz embodied the culture industry's unbearable depravity, and yet because of its means of distribution, through radio and the record industry, it became more than another genre—it was a genuine craze, unprecedented in the enthusiasm it provoked. Jazz created new dances and fashions, and it had an impact on family norms: the age of family sing-alongs and traditional formal dances was, for all intents and purposes, over.

Jazz revealed a paradox: in the age of mass communication a cultural force could be both wildly disruptive and wildly successful. And—at least for the moment—that cultural force could be critical and interrogative; it could celebrate independence. Culture was powerful, in other words, but it didn't seem to be in the hands of the powerful themselves. Or at any rate, not yet.

CERTAINLY THE NAZIS UNDERSTOOD THAT CULTURE IS A WEAPON

> The art of propaganda consists precisely in being able to awaken the imagination of the public through an appeal to their feelings, in finding the appropriate psychological form that will arrest the attention and appeal to the hearts of the national masses. The broad masses of the people are not

made up of diplomats or professors of public ju-
risprudence nor simply of persons who are able
to form reasoned judgment in given cases, but a
vacillating crowd of human children who are con-
stantly wavering between one idea and another.

—ADOLF HITLER, *Mein Kampf*

If these words sound very similar to the inklings of George
Creel and Walter Lippmann, it is because the idea was en
vogue (and perhaps even true). Manipulation of the un-
thinking masses had become a given for any rising-star
politician, and Hitler manipulated by any means necessary. For him, and the rest of Germany, the sting of the loss
of World War I was a powerful motivating force. Hitler
wanted to correct mistakes, including changing the methodology of the propaganda campaigns. While the Nazi
party took time to develop a popular platform, from the
beginning Hitler's political thinking rested heavily on a
long list of enemies. They were everywhere: bolsheviks,
gays, artists, and Jews remained the threat from within,
and the forces that had fought them in World War I were
the threat from outside. And they became the target of the
Reich's propaganda.

Not unlike the fervent homophobia of Jesse Helms,
the anti-Semitism of Adolph Hitler sprung from a deeply
held belief. By the end of World War I, Hitler, like many
Germans in the postwar trauma, held a deep conviction
that Jews were responsible for backstabbing the German
people. Irrational, yes, but extant nevertheless.

To call Hitler obsessively anti-Semitic is so obvious :hat historically *Hitler* has become synonymous with *anti-Semitism*. But as we can see in the story so far, many of the toolsets from which Hitler culled were already in the air (and continue to be so). Rather than an aberration, Hitler's rise to power came as a catalytic crescendo of the forces of culture as they combined the growing techniques of public relations and advertising with the burgeoning technology of cultural distribution. Mix all that with Hitler's rabid racism and one gets a historically unprecedented powder keg. The Aryan nation rolled through Deutschland like a precapitalist rock concert.

Even though Hitler was rejected by the Vienna Academy of Fine Arts in 1907 and again in 1908, he always possessed a deep belief in design, aesthetic, and poetics. His sensibility was innately operatic. He excelled in excess in everything, not only in rhetorical flourishes. His sense of aesthetics would become a signature feature of the Nazi party. After World War I, in 1919, he joined the German Workers Party (which would become the National Socialist German Workers Party [NSDAP], which would become the Nazi Party). Drawn particularly to their anticommunist, anticapitalist, nationalist ideology, Hitler soon redesigned their flag with the black swastika in a white circle on a blood-red background. Hitler writes in *Mein Kampf*: "The question of the new flag—that is, its appearance—occupied us intensely in those days. From all sides came suggestions . . . the new flag had to be equally a symbol of our own struggle, since on the other hand it was expected also to be highly effective as a poster . . . an effective insignia can in hundreds of thousands of cases give the first impetus towards interest in a movement." The swastika had already been in great circulation during the period, and Hitler was determined that his party have a flag more red, brilliant, and striking than their communist competitors. Hitler found himself in not only a political struggle, but also an aesthetic one. And he was determined to win.

The virulently anti-Semitic sycophant Joseph Goebbels famously and adeptly abetted Hitler in mobilizing propaganda. Rising up in the ranks to become head of Hitler's Reich Ministry of Public Enlightenment and Propaganda, Goebbels fancied himself a writer, philosopher, and public speaker. With a degree in philosophy from the University of Heidelberg, he eagerly penned speeches that detailed his philosophy on the great Aryan race, the rising tide of bolshevism coming out of Russia and at home, and the list of wrongs perpetuated by the Jews. Like Hitler, Goebbels was an orator and practiced his speeches in front of the mirror. Inflammatory speeches were a major part of his propaganda arsenal, and his most trusted companion was the same one as that of jazz: the radio.

Radio brought Nazi words into the living rooms of Germans. A movement that was simultaneously anti-intellectual yet deeply committed to public speaking, the Nazi party desired most of all an intimate connection with the human ear. During the Depression, when all seemed lost, the stirring words of Hitler and Goebbels would come on and send a bolt of electricity through the listener. As the economy lagged, German radio began to act as a vehicle by which one could locate enemies and salvation. "We live in the age of the masses; the masses rightly demand that they participate in the great events of the day. The radio is the most influential and important intermediary between a spiritual movement and the nation, between the idea and the people."[32] So wrote Goebbels.

While radio might have been Goebbels favorite technology, he possessed numerous forms for galvanizing support for the Nazi party. The Nazis never lacked a P. T. Barnum sense of showmanship. Starting in 1923, the NSDAP held massive stadium rallies with speeches, banners, and Wagnerian music. They held their first mega-rally in Munich, but they moved the second rally in 1927 to Nuremberg. It was a calculated move made with a sense of site specificity. Nuremberg became the home to the rallies as the medieval backdrop of the town itself provided the proper atmosphere for catalyzing a massive onslaught of nationalist hysteria. History spoke through the rubbled ground, through the distinct Bavarian architecture and the wooded hills. These massive events acted as an incantation of the spirit the likes of which the arts could never achieve, because even by the early twentieth century, they had all developed that un-German, and frankly unworldly, trait of skepticism. But for the Nazi youth, and there were many, these rallies proved primarily cathartic. The romantic capacity to not think critically was perhaps at an all-time high and even more so in a country that had been beaten down by war and was at the same time flooded with the new mechanisms of mass culture and advertising. It hit them in the face.

The rallies were deeply choreographed affairs chalk full of impassioned nationalist speeches and occult-like rituals for the growing Aryan nation. At the end of each rally, a ceremony called the "consecration of the colors" took place, whereby the new Nazi flags would touch the supposedly bloodstained flag of those killed in Hitler's failed military coup, the Beer Hall Putsch, of 1923.

In a bureaucratic demonstration of ambition, the scale and pageantry inevitably grew exponentially. An Aryan nation–style rock opera on par with Woodstock, the Olympics, and an Iron Maiden concert, the rallies gradually became an integral part of the Nazi propaganda machine. With Nuremberg becoming the ongoing site for the rallies, the architect of the party, Albert Speer, was commissioned to design the grounds. At the height of Nazi fever, Speer came up with the idea of utilizing the antiaircraft searchlights and producing what he called the "cathedral of light." These lights—all 130 of them—were shot directly up into the night sky, producing a spectacle that could be seen from miles around. More than theater, Speer had created a totalizing phantasmagoria. To say it was an art piece would undermine what it truly was: Speer created a spell.

These rallies were captured in film most famously by Nazi-propagandist filmmaker Leni Riefenstahl, particularly in her epic *Triumph of the Will* (1935). Considered to be the greatest propaganda film of all time, it documented the

1935 Nuremberg rally which featured 700,000 attendees. She utilized numerous innovative cinematic features, including aerial shots and shots taken with the camera moving. Before anything Nazi-related would be equated with evil and Refinstall with it, she received the gold medal in Venice for the film.

By 1933, as Goebells ascended to the head of propaganda and Hitler to chancellor, the entire spectrum of cultural apparatus became centralized in the government. The film industry, in particular, became nationalized as Goebbels was intent on consolidating and deploying this powerful tool of the moving image. It is estimated that 45 million German people watched these government-produced features.[33]

Ever the shunned artist, Hitler would exact his revenge in the production of the Great German Art Exhibition. Intended to highlight the kind of art that fit with the approval of the Nazi regime, the jury was initially organized by Goebbels. As art was a subject dear to Hitler's heart, it should be no surprise that when he saw what the jury selected, he had them all fired and started, again, from scratch with his own jurist, photographer Heinrich Hoffmann.

The slight to Goebbels only made the propaganda minister all the more creative. In a move that prefigures Jesse Helms, Goebbels concocted the basis for a simultaneous art show titled the *Degenerate Art* exhibition. It would feature German art that presented the degenerate spirit and the seeds of culture that were rotting the country from the inside out. It is hard to imagine Helms concocting such a thing, but at the same time, one can't help but think that

Helms had curated these shows in his mind. The *Degenerate Art* exhibition featured 650 works of art, including those by German Dadaist Georg Grosz, Wassily Kandinsky, Piet Mondrian, and Marc Chagall. The show drew massive crowds of nearly 20,000 people a day. Lacking in all irony, the Nazi party also considered it a success.

The Nazis loved culture. They used culture. They distributed culture. Cinema, music, flags, banners, book burnings, rallies, and holidays were all deployed in a phantasmagoria of stark blood red, swastikas, and blinding white. While certainly all this is known (anti-Semitism, propaganda, and Nazis are often synonymous in the post–World War II era), it is productive to view it in light of the mid-twentieth century's rapidly expanding culture industry. These phenomena were not individuated things; the cocktail of anti-Semitism, propaganda, and Nazis, combined with the growing techniques of culture, exploded to produce one of the largest meltdowns of that thing we call humanity.

Certainly there existed a social and political economy dimension to the landscape of Germany itself that paved the way for World War II and its holocaust. But the capacity to galvanize a population with the assistance of not only cultural manipulation but also, and more important, the emerging tools of cultural distribution made for a fertile terrain to coalesce a national psyche. Relentless Nazi anti-Semitism that made its way into every space was a powerful device to mobilize culture, with its connected devices of film, radio, print, design, and speech. The Nazis utilized the powerful device of the enemy to produce a nation. The enemy was a fulcrum for cultural manipulation and that enemy would end up being, as is known, placed into camps and murdered.

The Holocaust punctuated the end of the mid-twentieth century in a cloud of dread and doubt. Hitler as a figure became almost mythical. Bigger than life, the reputation of the Nazis and Hitler himself became so specifically exceptional that for many parts of the world the answer was to simply enjoy their victory. If anything, the lesson of the Holocaust became one of fearing the power of not only tyranny but also mob mentality. Writing on the trial of Adolph Eichmann, the Secret Service officer responsible for deporting Jews to the ghettos and concentration camps, philosopher Hannah Arendt writes, "Despite all the efforts of the prosecution, everybody could see that this man was not a 'monster,' but it was difficult indeed not to suspect that he was a clown. And since this suspicion would have been fatal to the entire enterprise, and was also rather hard to sustain in view of the sufferings he and his like had caused to millions of people, his worst clowneries were hardly noticed and almost never reported." Arendt's words spoke for many in the intellectual community. The most troubling aspect of the Nazis was not only the mob mentality, but also the sheer capacity to follow with conviction without much criticality at all. Like lemmings, the German people had collectively jumped off a cliff together into the torpid madness of their leader. Clowns all.

3

THE PERSUADERS, PART II

In the United States, the war years were marked by rationing, belt-tightening, and modesty. It was a kind of patriotic frugality, all for the sake of victory. The postwar era marked something of a release. Here was a new kind of consumption—grander in scale and more expansive in possibility. The culture and advertising industries, too, grew bigger than ever: they would shape, determine, and encourage American consumption for decades to come.

As we've seen, governments in the first half of the century had learned how to unleash PR and advertising with unprecedented sophistication and—at least in the case of the Nazis—unprecedented insidiousness. In the second half the century, those efforts were democratized: in the postwar era, the uses of culture were no longer only material for the state, they also became essential tools to be deployed by every business, no matter its scale or function.

Each branch of the military had a marketing department, but so did the grocery-store chain and, in many cases, the local bank. Commerce became inseparable from the forces of PR itself.

At the same time, immaterial goods took on a new degree of importance in the United States' economic and cultural life. Not only did television, music, film, fashion, and advertising come to play an enormous role in the domestic economy, but also—crucially—they would prove essential to Americans' understanding of the world around them. Culture was everywhere, and it radically altered the texture of daily life in the United States.

But paradoxically, even as its methods grew in size and sophistication, culture nonetheless succeeded in encouraging our national obsession with individuality and self-expression. The beatniks and Alan Ginsberg extolled liberation and independence, but so, too, did Madison Avenue. In other words, a generation's pursuit of its own identity had assistance and encouragement from the institutions that seemed, at first, like its classic antagonists. It's hard to imagine a better metaphor for the impact of culture and marketing than the selling of individuality and its relationship to acquisitiveness. In the second half of the twentieth century and into the twenty-first, could you really stand out if you didn't possess the consumer goods that would make you unique?

MOTHS TO THE LIMELIGHT

In 1941, the German Marxist Theodor Adorno arrived in Pacific Palisades, which had become, in the words of Thomas Mann, a kind of German California. The growing film industry (and its occasional left-wing sympathies) garnered the interest and incredulity of Germany's diasporic left-wing intelligentsia: by the time Adorno landed, Bertolt Brecht and Arnold Schoenberg were already on the scene, along with Mann himself.

Like Brecht, Adorno quickly realized that everything about Hollywood was antithetical to his own critical project. Adorno took aim at what he and fellow academic Max Horkheimer referred to as "the culture industry," which is best summarized in a chapter from their book, *Dialectic of Enlightenment* titled "The Culture Industry: Enlightenment as Mass Deception."

The essay illuminates the growing confluence between public relations, advertising, and the emerging technologies that distributed them. If George Gallup was interested in measuring public opinion, Adorno and Horkheimer posited that the entirety of these efforts was for the expansion of a consumer market:

> The assembly-line character of the culture industry, the synthetic, planned method of turning out its products (factory-like not only in the studio but, more or less, in the compilation of cheap biographies, pseudo-documentary novels, and hit songs) is very suited to advertising: the

important individual points, by becoming detachable, interchangeable, and even technically alienated from any connected meaning, lend themselves to ends external to the work. The effect, the trick, the isolated repeatable device, have always been used to exhibit goods for advertising purposes, and today every monster close-up of a star is an advertisement for her name, and every hit song a plug for its tune. Advertising and the culture industry merge technically as well as economically. In both cases the same thing can be seen in innumerable places, and the mechanical repetition of the same culture product has come to be the same as that of the propaganda slogan. In both cases the insistent demand for effectiveness makes technology into psycho-technology, into a procedure for manipulating men. In both cases the standards are the striking yet familiar, the easy yet catchy, the skillful yet simple; the object is to overpower the customer, who is conceived as absent-minded or resistant.[34]

Adorno and Horkheimer were concerned with how capitalism was shaping daily life, and thus they focused not only on culture, but also on the machines that produced it. The production of culture, they argued, couldn't help but produce a homogenizing affect, which reduced all cultural expression to the same filtered product. This product was easy to consume, but its reward wasn't purely aesthetic—ultimately, the object was commercial success, rather than quality.

For Adorno, this commercialization was hardly an abstract concern. An admirer of Schoenberg and modern experimental music, Adorno loathed the massification of culture: he found jazz particularly repellent and mainstream, but his disdain for popular culture cut across genre. (Living down the road from child star Shirley Temple probably didn't help matters.) Like many other avant-gardists, Adorno wrote off music and culture that were designed for the masses—as he saw it, all of it amounted to little more than commercials for the docile.

To say that this perspective had its blind spots is an understatement. Indeed, that jazz was one of America's greatest and most complex art forms was obvious to many at the time. But more broadly, the relentless emphasis on culture as a capitalist enterprise can't account for . . . well, joy. What is Motown or early rock and roll—or Willie Nelson or Fleetwood Mac—if not a wondrous phantasmagoria of spirited self-transformation and expression? To be as dour as Adorno about the culture industries means that one would have to reduce, say, D.C. hardcore to something much less than it was (which was absolutely amazing), or pretend that death metal isn't exhilaratingly terrifying. It means avoiding the greatness of Run-D.M.C. and Kendrick Lamar and everyone who has made any art that resonated with more than a handful of people. While one can and should be cynical about the role that capitalism has played in the emergence of the culture industries, one must also temper that cynicism with a deep appreciation for—and righteous belief in—the treasures that mainstream art has brought.

We should bear all of this in mind, even though, to a large extent, the critique holds. By the time Adorno and

Horkheimer offered their critiques, cinema had become a major American export. For much of the first half of the century, the big six film companies dominated the industry. Columbia Pictures, Universal Pictures, Paramount Pictures, Walt Disney Pictures, Warner Brothers Pictures, and 20th Century Fox not only made films, but they also produced the film stars, owned the distribution channels, and controlled the movie theaters. There is, perhaps, no greater sign of the industry's dominance—and no greater validation of Adorno's argument—than the fact that the man Hollywood had recruited to gauge public enthusiasm for films of the era was none other than our old friend George Gallup. Everyone from Orson Welles to Ginger Rogers was, to a large extent, market tested.

But the golden era of the film industry was also a deeply centralized one, and in the 1950s, the double whammy of an antitrust suit and the emergence of television knocked the industry back. Attendance dropped significantly in the 1950s: from 60 million in 1950 to 40 million in 1960.[35] Still, the film giants weren't going to cede cultural control without a struggle: they invested heavily in the television and music industries, ensuring that in one way or another, film remained dominant.

On October 29, 1952, Charlie Chaplin, the celebrated hero of silent cinema, hosted a press conference in Paris for *Lime Light*, the new film he wrote, directed, and starred in. Claire Bloom plays a suicidal dancer down on her luck who is nurtured back into health and confidence on the stage by an equally washed-up stage clown, Chaplin. At the end of the film, Chaplin performs a benefit concert with a fellow performer once thought lost to time played by Buster Keaton, only to suffer a heart attack as the dancer ends the performance to rave reviews. *Lime Light* is a comeback film that ends in tragedy, and it's hard not to see it as a metaphor: a story about the changing of the guard in Hollywood.

The press conference didn't go well for Chaplin. For all his fame and glory, Chaplin had remained a darling of the left for his consistent portrayals of the down-and-out and the working-class man. But a young, radical fringe had singled him out as a convenient target—and decided to use a mass-media opportunity to critique the power of mass media. Members of a group calling themselves Lettrists descended on his Paris press conference with leaflets in hand that stated "NO MORE FLAT FEET." The accompanying text read in part, "Because you've identified yourself with the weak and oppressed, to attack you is to attack the weak and oppressed—but in the shadow of your rattan cane some could already see the nightstick of a cop."[36] They were outing Chaplin as a phony. A rich man capitalizing on the image of poverty. Chaplin was blindsided and unprepared.

The group evolved into an even more radical outfit, and in 1957, the younger cadre formed a new group called the Situationists International that was fiercely anti–pop culture and pro–avant-garde (and pro-Marxism). Their most prominent spokesperson, Guy Debord, was a petulant type with a fierce intelligence and little patience for idiocy. The Situationsts were particularly concerned with what they called "advanced capitalism"—the production of people's tastes and desires through marketing and cultural pro-gramming—and Debord would go on to write *Society of the Spectacle*, one of the most influential (and vicious) critiques of media culture.

But the encounter with Chaplin wasn't simply a matter of an internal rupture within an avant-garde organization: it is, in many ways, a perfect symbol of the era's defining tendency toward distrust of mainstream culture. What was a fringe opinion in 1952 was a dominant intellectual cur-rent by the late 1960s, when the Situationists' unforgiving analysis and totalizing distrust translated to a generational mood. Their critique of visual culture and its collusion with capitalism struck a chord with the insurrectionists of 1968 Paris, who covered Paris with graffiti and pamphlets riddled with classic Situationist phraseology, "Under the sidewalk, the beach!," "Never work," and "We don't want a world where the guarantee of not dying of starvation brings the risk of dying of boredom."

THE SOUND OF FREEDOM

But widespread skepticism toward mass culture hardly meant immunity from culture, generally. A year after the 1968 uprising in Paris and elsewhere, a three-day mu-sic festival on a dairy farm in Woodstock, New York, cemented the marriage between youth and music. Many young Americans were in a rebellious mood, but it wasn't easy to tease apart the growing appetite for music with the equally growing appetite for freedom, liberation, and self-defining. After all, by 1969, music was big business—in many was as dominant as film had been earlier in the century. Woodstock concert promoter Michael Lang went so far as to describe Woodstock as a "relaxed" way to bring entrepreneurs together. The spirit of the creative industries already existed then. And certainly, the numbers were there to prove it. And so, despite its many virtues, Woodstock helped exploit a growing youth appetite for music and culture targeted largely at itself.

Music wasn't a microwave or a washing machine; it was barely tactile—it was endless and shape-shifting and, as the years went on, endlessly replicable. You don't need to believe in a clear relationship between culture and ideas—or culture and personality—to understand that a force that so affected an impressionable population would have an impact on every aspect of American life. In the 1960s, music was both a consumer good and much more than a consumer good; it was a cultural force of unprecedented influence. In the years to come, the economy would increasingly be organized around immaterial goods and a seemingly never-ending interest in self-articulation.

Music stirred the hearts of not only the United States' youth, but would also become an essential element of how America looked at itself in the mirror. Publicly, billboard charts could reflect the hit songs of the era, and privately, one could close one's eyes and hear it. Songs could speak simultaneously to one person while also to millions. More than just something to listen to, music had become something to shape oneself to. It was both out there and in here, jumbling around in the head. The financial growth of the music industry only tells part of the story: for while money is an indicator and shaper of an industry, it doesn't tell what you sing while in the shower. It is reasonable to assume that for every band that made money, five others did not. For every song bought, countless hours were spent at night crying over a lost relationship or whistling at work. Even if an album is purchased just once, it can be played hundreds upon thousands of times. Like a turntable, the music can just keep on playing. The United States not only gained an ever-shifting theme song, it also gained a new way of occupying its citizens' time and dreams.

The 1960s and '70s watched this massive population of baby boomers become fascinated, hypnotized, and of course, purchasing, the images, music, and clothes that would come to define them. Entertainment spending already by 1960 was at a massive $85 billion.[37] It was the dawn of what would come to be described as the "service and information economy." Consumer goods were clearly no longer material things, but instead intangible, immaterial cultural things. Self-articulation not only came with beatnik poems scribbled in books, but also with purchased albums and clothes—which would mean big business.

THE BOOB TUBE

And then there was TV. Between 1949 and 1969, the number of households with a television rose from less than 1 million to 44 million. The family that once gathered around the radio in the living room switched to the big box without hesitation. Throughout the 1960s, the most dominant, efficient, and pervasive culture-distributing technology yet invented muscled its way into every household. TV was king.

Television came of age in the 1960s, and the history of that decade is inseparable from the history of its most central medium. Think of the televised debate between the telegenic John F. Kennedy and the sweating, frumpy Richard Nixon—a political event that unquestionably revealed television's true power. Or the Kennedy assassination, only three years later: more efficiently than any radio broadcast or newspaper, television showed that it could circulate the emotions of shock and horror; one could step outside and know the person staring off into the sky across the street had just seen the same thing.

The upheavals of the 1960s resonated in the public consciousness to the extent that they did because of television. It's impossible to imagine the indelible victories of the civil rights era without the distribution of much horrific, moving, visceral footage: black high-school students attacked by dogs and blasted by fire hoses during the Birmingham campaign, Martin Luther King, Jr.'s major speeches—the list is long.

Yet it's not only a high-minded story. Music didn't merely inspire, connect, and radicalize, and television didn't merely inspire and foment social change. Self-evidently not. Suddenly, given the television's omnipresence, advertising had more power than ever before: the explosion of a medium of vast visual communication held great promise for Madison Avenue. Throughout the 1950s, advertising grew as a phenomenon: its revenues shot up from to $12 billion by 1960.

But before we delve back into the world of the advertisers, we need to spend some time with some of the era's great seers.

THE SEERS

More than fellow beat poets like Allen Ginsberg and Jack Kerouac, William Burroughs possessed a keen awareness of the changing media landscape. Less an analyst than a historic clairvoyant, Burroughs could feel the shifts at the edge of his skin. Unlike the Situationists, who expressed only antipathy for mass culture, Burroughs possessed a profound respect for the liberatory capacity of modern media. "The media are really accessible to everyone," he wrote. "People talk about establishment media, but the establishment itself would like to suppress the media altogether."[38] Burroughs went as far as to argue that the social upheavals of the late 1960s owed less to the movement of people in the streets than to the power of media and its ability to create new associations and meanings and identities:

> The past 40 years has seen a worldwide revolution without precedent owing to the mass media which has cursed and blessed us with immediate worldwide communication. Everything that happens anywhere now happens everywhere on the TV screen. I am old enough to remember when the idea that Gays, Hispanics, and Blacks had any rights at all was simply absurd. A Black was a nigger, a Hispanic was a spic and a Gay was a fucking queer. And that was that. Tremendous progress has been made in leading ordinary people to confront these issues which now crop up in soap operas. Gay and junky are household words. Believe me, they were not household words 40 years ago.[39]

If Adorno worried that the culture industries could only be counted on to produce cookie-cutter personalities, Burroughs saw them as spaces of vast social production. More culture meant more cultural possibilities. Burroughs was fascinated with the connections between words and image. Like a contemporary ad man, he loved the associative world of desire and image and text that defined commercial television. Burroughs was deeply skeptical of the idea of human rationality, and as such he saw these associations as absolutely key to the human mind. Burroughs believed that people thought in terms of what he called "association blocks," and in his pulpy, surreal books *Nova Express* and

Naked Lunch, he wrote in streams of associative language. Burroughs was also, poetically enough, the nephew of public-relations founder Ivy Lee.

At the same time, a Burroughs corollary emerged in the art world, which was growing and commercializing at a rapid pace. For all his eventual fame, fortune, glamour, and renown, Andy Warhol was a peculiar, hugely perceptive barometer of the media barrage that had flooded American life. Like any good artist, Warhol worked from what he saw and knew: having gotten his start in commercial design, Warhol culled from the growing visual culture that surrounded him. His subsequent elevation of Pop into Art derived from an acute awareness that the sands of culture had shifted. The marriage between culture and capitalism that Adorno feared was greeted by Andy Warhol with open arms.

While Warhol shared Burroughs's fascination with and respect for the media sphere—and advertising, in particular—he differed from Burroughs in his wholesale embrace of consumerism. A good antagonist, Burroughs wrote about thought police and mechanisms of control, whereas Warhol simply took it all in with a kind of confounding equanimity. Warhol loved money, commercials, television, fame, and many of the forces that lurked at the center of American capitalist life. He embraced that which the century's great avant-gardes had found most harmful.

Warhol's art—like Burroughs's—was oracular. He revealed the many contradictions and shifts that had become palpable in a relatively short amount of time. Media had come to dominate contemporary life, divisions between high and low culture were fading, and consumer logic had begun to infiltrate vast sectors of everyday life. In many ways, what Adorno and Horkheimer had described only twenty years earlier had come to pass.

MADISON AVENUE

If, as Warhol and Burroughs sensed, a revolution was transforming the distribution of culture, the field of advertising—one of that revolution's main beneficiaries—was also in a state of upheaval. Increased consumerism and the rise of new mediums that would help spread the word (and image) on a national and global scale were at the heart of what is known as advertising's "creative revolution." Public relations may have dominated the landscape of the early twentieth century, but in the mid-twentieth century, advertising ruled.

David Ogilvy is an unlikely protagonist in the history of advertising. He began his advertising career relatively late at the age of thirty-eight. A disciple of George Gallup, Ogilvy worked with the Intelligence Service at the British embassy in Washington, D.C., where he suggested using Gallup's survey techniques in the psychological operations of the war. After the war, Ogilvy made a name for himself with two memorable advertisements. In 1951, he produced a national campaign for Hathaway Company, a Maine-based shirt company. Equipped with little more than his innate sense for the catchy, Ogilvy hired a debonair, mustached model whom he clothed with the shirts in question—and a single eye patch. An image at once comical and sophisticated (the latter reinforced by Ogilvy's decision to advertise only in *The New Yorker*), it was irresistible: the Hathaway shirt man became a sensation.

After the Hathaway shirt man came Commander Edward Whitehead. Ogilvy recruited the president of Schweppes, Edward Whitehead—a British naval officer and a veteran of the South Pacific campaign—for the campaign, which portrayed Schweppes (and, by extension, all Schweppes drinkers) as an elegant gentleman: part adventurer, part sophisticate. The Schweppes commander again was a smash hit—a brand icon.

If Ogilvy was a master off the offbeat, the rumpled, pudgy, horn-rimmed Leo Burnett triumphed by producing ads that were folksy and affable. A midwesterner through and through, Burnett was a tireless worker who sought to convey simple truths through advertising. "None of us," he told executives in 1955, "can underestimate the glacier-like power of friendly familiarity."[40] Burnett's campaign for Kellogg's was a perfect example of this approach. Cereal— perhaps the blandest food on the market—was radically altered in the public imagination by the introduction of an iconic figure, Tony the Tiger, and Burnett's decision to conceive of the cereal box as a canvas for spectacular colors and relentless brand identity. Burnett also showed himself to be the rightful heir to Bernays in the realm of tobacco advertising. The latter had made Lucky Strike a cigarette for suffragettes, but the former accomplished nothing less than the transformation of Marlboro into the number one brand in the world. The Marlboro Man is perhaps advertising's most iconic image.

Is it possible to compare the work of Ogilvy and Burnett to the art of Warhol and Burroughs and Dada? It's not an intuitive connection, I realize, but all of them—the advertisers and the artists—understood the power of the visual, the evocative, the emotive, and the associative. All of them were fundamentally concerned with new, more efficient, and more radical modes of production and distribution.

Still, even if one were to put all qualitative distinctions between art and advertising aside, the major differences between the two are scale and mission. These artists did not produce work that could exist within newspapers, magazines, radio, and television—no matter their contemporaneity, their work remained niche, reaching limited audiences versus the mass culture of popular cinema and television. And despite some shared philosophical conceptions, their motives were totally dissimilar: Burroughs, Warhol, and the Dadaists all sought to create new associations that would disrupt people's expectations of traditional idioms—they were ahead of their time, while Ogilvy and Burnett wanted to use those expectations to their fullest potential.

This isn't to say, though, that all advertising of the time was safe, or simply aimed at reinforcing status quos. Take

Doyle, Dane, and Bernbach's (DDB) radical campaign for Volkswagen in the late 1950s: an advertising campaign about advertising. The ads for the VW Beetle were stark and cheap and black and white—worlds away from the lush, colorful campaigns for other cars (and consumer goods) of the era. But it was the words that were really shocking: LEMON, UGLY, and THINK SMALL. Here were ads that were ironic and irreverent and self-deprecating: Americans who believed in skepticism and opposition to the system now had a car that embodied the same spirit. As a generation began to define itself by its distance from the mainstream, advertising often led the way.

And again, advertising wasn't simply selling consumer goods. After their triumph with the Beetle, DDB created the infamous Daisy ad for Lyndon Johnson's campaign against Barry Goldwater. In the ad, a young girl counts the petals she picks from a daisy. She counts slowly, and when she finally pulls the last petal off, the camera zooms into her face while the audio switches to the countdown of a nuclear bomb. The next images are of a massive nuclear explosion, followed by the words, "We must love each other or we must die. Vote for Lyndon Johnson this November 3. The stakes are too high for you to stay home." The advertisement made clear how dangerous the right-wing Goldwater would be. (Incidentally, Goldwater's advertisements were created by Leo Burnett.) Coercive to the extreme, the ad was nonetheless hugely effective.

For all its innovations, though, the advertising industry wasn't keeping pace with one key aspect of American life: the growing recognition of identities other than the dominant ones. But soon, the Mad Men caught up. Advertising's answer to a more diverse, more hyphenated United States was market segmentation. As Thomas Frank writes in his insightful book *The Conquest of Cool*, "Postwar American capitalism was hardly the unchanging and soulless machine imagined by countercultural leaders; it was as dynamic a force in its own way as the revolutionary youth movements of the period, undertaking dramatic transformations of both the way it operated and the way it imagined itself."[41]

THE REVOLUTION AND THE CEREAL BOX

By the late 1960s, media critiques weren't being voiced by angry Germans in Pacific Palisades or barging into press conferences unannounced—critiques were approaching the mainstream. For all its massive popularity and cultural dominance, the TV was being subjected to an entirely new degree of criticism: the source of music and entertainment and glorious advertising was now a brainwashing box. The era's ascendant subcultures and liberation movements took on mass communication as a central antagonist: "I do not expect the white media to create positive black male images," said Black Panthers founder Huey Newton. Television was suburban, regressive, racist, patriarchal. In September 1968, the Miss America pageant in Atlantic City was disrupted by the activist group, New York Radical Women (NYRA). NYRA targeted the schlocky beauty pageant for perpetuating the objectification of women, and its protestors proceeded to throw everything from fake eyelashes to mops to bras into a dumpster. In their ten-point manifesto, NYRA linked the growing mediated world to the waking, living one: "Miss America is a walking commercial for the Pageant's sponsors. Wind her up and she plugs your product on promotion tours and TV—all in an 'honest, objective' endorsement."[42]

But it wasn't all antagonistic. The backlash against the mainstream culture industry also took the form of new kinds of products—in many cases, the mechanisms of critique themselves took the form of culture. Take *Ms.* magazine, founded by Gloria Steinem and Dorothy Pitman Hughes in 1972, in reaction to the dominance of male-owned and -edited magazines. Women owned and women focused, *Ms.* magazine became a signpost for movements interested in producing their own media.

In the late 1960s and early '70s, examples of this kind abound—cultural backlash that was, in turn, an important contribution to culture. Gil Scott-Heron declared that the revolution wouldn't be televised on his album *Small Talk on 125th and Lenox*, and Sly and the Family Stone took on white power, war, and poverty on their album *Stand!*, which was released on Epic Records and sold 500,000 copies in its first year. The voices of liberation had gone national.

But the mainstream wasn't easily defeated. By the time Richard Nixon ran for office in 1968, he had learned many lessons since his failed debate with JFK. Nixon's chief of staff, H. R. Haldeman, had served twenty years at ad giant J. Walter Thompson, and a number of other aides were Thompson veterans as well. Which explains, in part, why the Nixon campaign was perhaps the most public-relations-dependent political campaign the United States had yet seen. More than ever, spin was an end in itself.

And as an unprecedented degree of market segmentation, consumer research, and PR led Nixon to the White House, the tools of marketing and commerce would come to dominate American life. Antagonism and rebellion were big business, but increasingly, culture was *everyone's* business. The transformation of the American economy and the collapse of manufacturing are histories we know well, yet those stories' outcome is germane to the story of culture's ascent we're concerned with in this book. The shift to a service economy meant that culture had to be everywhere: immaterial goods were absolutely on the rise, and those goods needed personalities—they needed a message.

Just as Leo Burnett understood that his canvas was the entirety of the cereal box, the world at large had become the cereal box. In the final third of the twentieth century, advertising would insert itself into every facet of daily life, and more than ever, where packaging ended and the product began was anyone's guess.

And while Adorno could afford to distinguish high and low, culture and commerce, art and garbage, no credible observer of the late twentieth century would be able to do the same. The culture of rebellion, which seemed like it could stand apart, even as it fell prey to marketing, had become another form of commerce: raw material for marketers looking to embrace antagonism and nostalgia.

Culture was everywhere, and because it was everywhere, it had an enormous impact on our lives. The torrent of advertising and PR that unleashed itself onto the world couldn't help but shape that world. This isn't to say that before the twentieth century, or before World War II, or before the 1960s, we found ourselves in some exalted age of reason. Surely not. But the increased scale changed everything.

Burroughs was right, and so was Bernays: we live in a world of affect and feeling, and it's impossible to overestimate the impact of culture writ large on every decision, every gesture, and every emotion. What follows in the next several chapters, then, are readings of different elements of modern life that begin with the understanding that culture and affect are everywhere—even in places where we don't necessarily expect to find them. My goal is not to revel in our collective irrationality, or to make a case for the bought-ness or corruption of all our institutions; rather, I want to identify the ways culture makes itself felt, and the way affect is used to sell and exploit. By paying close attention to the way culture wends itself through our world, I hope to rebut the popular understanding that capital and politics are separate from culture, rather than intimately linked to it.

4

FEAR MACHINES

When FDR stated in 1933, "The only thing we have to fear is fear itself," his words echoed as prophetic as they were fatalistic. Meant as a balm to the growing hysteria over the social collapse of the Great Depression, the implications of his words linger as a lesson to political discourse itself:

> This great Nation will endure as it has endured, will revive and will prosper. So, first of all, let me assert my firm belief that the only thing we have to fear is fear itself—nameless, unreasoning, unjustified terror which paralyzes needed efforts to convert retreat into advance. In every dark hour of our national life a leadership of frankness and vigor has met with that understanding and support of the people themselves which is essential to victory. I am convinced that you will again give that support to leadership in these critical days.

Politics and fear have a long-standing relationship. And like many political speeches, this particularly affective one possesses a peculiar double meaning. The speech can soothe as well as be a testament to the profound powers of fear. Even mentioning fear evokes fear. In a cartoon by Gary Larson from his *The Far Side*, a dog stands by a door waiting for a mailman. As everyone knows, dogs can smell your fear. The mailman gingerly walks toward the door, eyes fixated on the dog, as the dog points back at the mailman a device with an antenna labeled FEAR METER. The mailman is stuck in a laughable and tragic dilemma. He cannot show fear or he will be ravaged by the dog, but the fear of showing fear is already a fear itself. Having only fear to fear is frankly not comforting. And yet, ultimately, it is also the tragic condition we face today. Fear is not only a difficult emotion to resist, it is equally a difficult political tool to stand against.

You cannot tell the story about the rise of culture and affect and marketing without discussing fear. We tend to think of selling and production as gestures tinged with positivity: surely it's more effective to persuade than to unnerve. But we must only remember the Daisy ad from the previous chapter—fear works, and it has always worked.

And as culture has taken on a dominant role in our lives, so has fear. In this chapter, unlike the others, I want to focus on a raw human emotion. Fear has supremacy on the spectrum of emotional responses, and by focusing on fear, we can put into conversation a series of what are seemingly disparate phenomena. And rather than simply focus on these phenomena's economic, sociological, or even historic underpinnings, a focus on fear in light of the deployment of culture will allow us to appreciate the powerful uses of affect, particularly fear, can be.

A fundamental turning point in the story of the ascent of fear is the 1988 U.S. presidential election.

JUST SAY NO AND THE NEW JIM CROW

During his campaign, George H. W. Bush promised a "kinder and gentler" approach to politics. Bush's campaign manager, however, wasn't a kinder and gentler type. Lee Atwater was an unholy mixture of Edward Bernays, Leo Burnett, and Burt Reynolds. He possessed an implicit understanding of vulnerabilities, and he lived for attacks.

Atwater probably never read Bernays, but he played his game intuitively. In *Crystalizing Public Opinion*, Bernays wrote, "The public relations counsel sometimes uses the current stereotype, combats them, and creates them. In using them he very often brings to the public he is reaching a stereotype they already know, to which he adds his new ideas, thus he fortifies his own, and thus gives greater carrying power."[43] In 1988 (and, for that matter, right now), white fear loomed large, and thus no stereotype was riper for exploitation than that of the scary black man. Hence, Willie Horton.

The Horton story—a convicted African American killer rapes a woman and kills her fiancé while on a Massachusetts furlough program supported by Michael Dukakis, the Democratic nominee—suited Atwater's needs perfectly. Dukakis hadn't invented the furlough program, but it didn't matter: even a minor interest in the concept of prison rehabilitation made the candidate vulnerable in the politics of fear. "By the time we're finished," Atwater said, "they're going to wonder whether Willie Horton is Dukakis's running mate." And sure enough, Horton was key to the Bush stump speech.

The infamous Horton ad, which aired in the fall of 1988, couldn't have been any more blatant. It was filmed to be scary and dramatic and, crucially, disavowable: Atwater and Bush could deny that the ad had anything to do with racism. That the ad was produced—and cowritten—by Roger Ailes, the only recently departed president of the Fox News channel, seems downright poetic. Ailes, a long-time political consultant and media man, had worked with the Reagan administration and Nixon. He understood intuitively what made news. "If you have two guys on a stage and one guy says, 'I have a solution to the Middle East problem,' and the other guy falls in the orchestra pit, who do you think is going to be on the evening news?" Simple as it seems, Ailes insights would go on to mold future news programming. The orchestra pit would come to be home to most of American politics. More than any American in the last thirty years, Ailes helped fear go mainstream.

Atwater and Ailes's dirty tricks weren't new—indeed, they were straight out of Nixon's southern strategy. Already in the 1960s, coded language—"bussing" or "states' rights"—

could stoke white fear more effectively than outright racism. And lest anyone doubt the particularity of the mission and the strategy, Atwater himself confirmed the intent. In a rare moment of candor, he was blunt about the motivations that made these fear-based strategies so effective:

> You start out in 1954 by saying, "Nigger, nigger, nigger." By 1968 you can't say "nigger"—that hurts you. Backfires. So you say stuff like forced busing, states' rights, and all that stuff. You're getting so abstract now [that] you're talking about cutting taxes, and all these things you're talking about are totally economic things and a byproduct of them is [that] blacks get hurt worse than whites. And subconsciously maybe that is part of it. I'm not saying that. But I'm saying that if it is getting that abstract, and that coded, that we are doing away with the racial problem one way or the other. You follow me—because obviously sitting around saying, "We want to cut this," is much more abstract than even the busing thing, and a hell of a lot more abstract than "Nigger, nigger."[44]

Coding, then, was as important as the racism itself—you could tap into white fear, but crucially, you could do it in a way that would let everyone off the hook from complicity.

And what happened when fear was deployed not merely in service of a presidential campaign, but toward an even bigger—and arguably more consequential—phenomenon? What happened, among other things, was the drug war, and the resultant "new Jim Crow," to use Michelle Alexander's formulation. As Alexander wrote in *The New Jim Crow*, "By waging a war on drug users and dealers, Reagan made good on his promise to crack down on the racially defined 'others'—the undeserving."[45]

Crime, drug use, and an underlying fear of black America combined to deliver the kind of spectacular sensationalism that news reports couldn't avoid. According to Alexander, "Between 1988 and October 1989, *The Washington Post* alone ran 1,565 stories about the 'drug scourge.'"[46] And while drug use extends across racial lines, the focus of criminalization was—unsurprisingly but devastatingly—black and brown. Statistics that revealed that white drug use equaled that of blacks had no impact on the systematic targeting, harassment, and imprisonment of young African Americans.

Of course, the ascent of the war on drugs wasn't the product of the news media alone—a number of culture industries also invested in selling the hype of the new black criminal. Culture, after all, doesn't work in isolation. The 1988 *Colors*, starring Sean Penn and Robert Duvall, sensationalized the deadly rivalry between the Crips and the Bloods in Los Angeles. N.W.A's landmark album *Straight Outta Compton* hit the shelves that same year. In 1991, Mario Van Peebles's *New Jack City*—starring Wesley Snipes, Ice-T, and Chris Rock—reinforced the image. The press ate it all up—and commercial success was inevitable. If communists were the enemy of the Cold War, the black gangster became the cultural enemy of the 1990s.

Again, not all unlike the war on the NEA or Tipper's

war on 2 Live Crew, the news media and politicians each got to weigh in on gangsta rap with the "cake and eat it too" approach of condemning while highlighting. Whether it was the war on drugs or the vilification of violent black music, the media sphere was abuzz with the sensationalism of this new genre. While speaking acrimoniously, politicians and news media also benefitted from the very aspects they would condemn. In the nelson ratings of attention spans, getting tough on crime, and thus evoking the black criminal, became the go-to political discourse. Michelle Alexander, weighing in on the 2016 Democratic primary, reminded the news media of Hillary Clinton's role in promoting her husband's three-strikes law. Pushing for faster measures that would eventually lead to the prison population explosion, Clinton opined in 1994, "There is something wrong when a crime bill takes six years to work its way through Congress and the average criminal serves only four. There is something wrong with our system."[47]

One could ask what is particularly new about saying that politics are racist? What is new is the sophistication and scale of industries that understand not only that culture is a powerful force, but also, and more important in this case, that fear is a more powerful emotion than most. Fear of the dangerous other gains profound traction across a wide spectrum of culture industries. Woe to the category of person that becomes the focus of that fear as a wide array of industries from music to politics to film to television consistently use that fear to garner attention. Thus, the role of the black male youth became a dominant figure in the mindset of mid-nineties America, and radio, television, film and politicians had much to do with the image's prominence.

CODE YELLOW

The war on drugs is by no means over, and the image of the black criminal remains depressingly persistent. Still, there's no better contemporary example of the deployment of fear than the Global War on Terror (GWOT).

In many ways, the Global War on Terror feels like the culmination of three decades in which the increased use of culture came to define political and social life. Here was a war waged—on the rhetorical level—against a human emotion in response to a sequence of events perfectly designed to produce fear. The orchestrators of the attacks of September 11 understood that to get attention was to acquire power. In an age saturated by cultural production, a mass tragedy created an extraordinary opportunity. And while the horrific violence remained fresh, a new specter emerged in the public consciousness: the Arab terrorist.

Fear wasn't just subtext, of course—it was addressed head-on, and stoked with unprecedented vigor. "I know many citizens have fears tonight," said President George W. Bush days after the attacks, "and I ask you to be calm and resolute, even in the face of a continuing threat."[48] It would be wrong to see this distinctly un-calming rhetoric as a slip of the tongue or a careless overreaction. In their

book *Selling Fear: Counterterrorism, the Media and Public Opinion,*
Brigitte L. Nacos, Yaeli Bloch-Elkon, and Robert Y. Shapiro write that "hyping threat and fear is central to terrorist
and counterterrorist rhetoric—it is part of a mass persua-
sion effort directed at audiences in whose interest terrorist
organizations and the governments in targeted countries
claim to act."[49] In other words, fear works. And it works
for all sides.

Here we return to the question of scale. Culture in
our time can be transmitted so quickly, so efficiently, and
so widely that fear immediately became inescapable. We
were a nation told to say something if we saw something, a
population in desperate need of updates from the "Terror
Watch" about the "Nation on Alert."

Permanent crisis was the dominant modality after 9/11,
and nothing embodied that spirit quite as well as the infamous terror-alert warning system, instituted by the newly
formed Department of Homeland Security. The terror
warnings had antecedents: the air-raid sirens that blasted
across Britain during World War II; the commercials in
the 1950s that warned of an impending atomic-bomb attack; the disruptive, eerie tests of radio's "emergency broadcasting system." But even at their shrillest, those alarms
were temporary and isolated. The terror alert system was
extreme at all times—an ongoing state of emergency.

Not everyone bought it, of course. Indeed, the deployment of fear throughout the GWOT served as the butt of
numerous jokes throughout the long Bush years. But those
jokes were all tinged with sadness, because everyone—critics

and supporters alike—bore witness to a simple fact: fear was persuasive and effective.

One of the most revealing examples of just how much of our public life was overtaken by fear in the post-9/11 era hits close to home. In 2004, my friend Steve Kurtz, a founding member of the political-art collective Critical Art Ensemble, awoke to find his wife and coartistic collaborator, Hope, dead of congenital heart failure. Kurtz dialed 911 for help, and when the paramedics arrived, they noticed a laboratory in the corner of the house. The first responders had been instructed to report any signs of potential bioterrorism to the authorities, and here was a laboratory in the home of a long-haired professor.

The freshly minted bioterrorism task force didn't have many cases to investigate, which is how Steve found himself being interrogated about the many questionable materials in his home, including a postcard for an art exhibition that had some Arabic writing on it. Kurtz's home was searched by FBI agents wearing hazardous material suits, which made for haunting, grainy local and national news footage: long-haired professor who has written about anarchism and liberation politics, under investigation by the feds. The fact that Kurtz was interested in genetically modified organisms and the implications of their uses in our food supply would have made for boring television. Instead, what the news media and politicians sought was the easy mythology of a weird scientist who happened to look like Ted Kaczynski possibly caught up in a movement of antigovernment anarchists. The district court pursued the case as it made headlines, and it wasn't until 2008 that Kurtz was cleared, when the presiding judge deemed the case "insufficient on its face."

I should add that Kurtz's story has a relatively happy ending. By 2008, the political mood had shifted, which helped matters considerably, and crucially, unlike those swept up in the prewar raids that brought suspected terrorists into the prisons of Guantanamo Bay (a tragic and tactile consequence of the fear era), Kurtz was an American, and a man with a constituency: he was an artist, and his fellow artists could (and did) support his case publicly and financially.

IF IT BLEEDS, IT LEADS

The experience of the last few years has shown that the media hardly needs fears as specific—or even as dominant—as 9/11 to perpetuate that sense of crisis. Given scale and instantaneity, any large-scale spectacle will do: the BP oil spill, the latest school shooting, the Ebola panic; the more destruction, death, and disease, the more attention.

Which means that it's not just color-coded terror reports that provoke overreach: what we've seen is a permanent dynamic of hyperbole. News must be gripping and provocative and narrative at all times, and god forbid if anyone tunes out. This kind of pattern is surely bad for our national health, but it's not merely our geopolitical enemies who take advantage of this cultural landscape—the public participates in the manufacture of culture, and can and does internalize these tendencies.

Sometimes with spectacular results. Just as the Lettrists used the mass-media spectacle of the Hollywood press conference to antagonize the mass media in 1952, a group of radicals used network news's techniques against them in Zuccotti Park in 2011. Occupy Wall Street was an act of physical resistance—the occupation of space with tremendous resonance—but the group's triumph went beyond the symbolic: it was deeply visual. Here were ready-made images in service of the destruction of our capitalist order: a YouTube video of a cop beating a defenseless, young protester or helicopter footage of a protest over the Brooklyn Bridge. The technique of perpetuating these images is known in the activist community as "riot porn"—it had emerged ten years earlier, during the alt-globalization movement. The familiar arrangement of tyrannical cops decked out with big guns and futuristic shields and facemasks made for good news. But the downside was self-evident: while these images circulated quickly and freely, when the story of the bad police and the righteous protestors wore thin (and all news stories inevitably do), the focus became a dirty camp in disarray.

Yet again, the images that received the most attention were those that played into a basic narrative of crowds, of chaos. The media has little time for complexity, and even less time for movements that look unfavorably on its own supremacy, as Occupy certainly did. In other words, the circulation of images that depicted violence and struggle failed to produce large-scale sympathy; here again, instead, was fear.

We've all heard the adage "If it bleeds, it leads"—the phrase has taken on the pervasiveness of a homily. But it is also true on a systemic level. In his book *The Culture of Fear*, the academic Barry Glassner emphasizes the serial exaggerations of our media age: plane crashes that stand in for an alleged epidemic of unsafety, special reports on crime that mask a rapidly falling crime rate, and on and on. Local news, in particular, is a cornucopia of horrifying tales, all of them with an implicit or explicit social message: it's scary out there. Glassner argues that to assess how completely our fear-based culture distorts the public mind, we need to reckon with something called the *availability heuristic*. The availability heuristic describes how people prioritize issues based on how relevant they are to their own lives. So as the news media hones in on the most terrifying and gruesome images, the public can't help but see the world in just this light. "The short answer to why Americans harbor so many misbegotten fears," Glassner writes, "is that immense power and money await those that tap into our moral insecurities and supply us with symbolic substitutes."[50] Rather than simply blaming the media or even politicians for perpetuating fear, it would make more sense to acknowledge that when it comes to grabbing attention, fear works.

FEAR AS BRICK AND MORTAR

The promulgation of fear certainly affects how people feel. Watching catastrophes, gun battles, and spreading disease on television inevitably shake up the viewers' psychology. But the effects of mass mobilized fear do not merely stay in the realm of human emotions. They also seep into the physical construction of the world around us. A world of vastly circulated fear will inevitably produce massive infrastructures with fear as their brick and mortar. While threats of terrorism or crime may be used for the sake of getting attention, they simultaneously inform funding, policies, and urban planning.

Nothing could make this point clearer than the exploding prison industry in the United States, and that extrajuridical camp located in Cuba named Guantanamo Bay. The dynamics of cultural manipulation are not only abstractions, they also become policies that become laws that become institutions that become infrastructures. In a landscape congested with media playing on symbols and toying with popular emotion and anxiety, the results are not just a broad-based confusion by the public on what is in their economic interest, but an entire economy and built environment produced by way of the real culture wars. Prisons are not made because they are profitable; in fact, the incarceration complex is exceptionally famous for being a total loser of money (perhaps with the exception of the prison guard's union). But yes, prisons are an industry, but not one explained by a basic sense of the promise of capitalism. Prisons are unequivocally the result of racist uses of fear.

And the same of course goes for Guantanamo Bay. A place outside of the actual landmass and rights of the United States, Gitmo became synonymous with a place to keep the worst of the worst in the war on terror. If Dick Cheney and Donald Rumsfeld believed that the 9/11 attacks produced enough emotional fuel to leverage a war in Iraq, the supposed terrorists locked up in Guantanamo were the living proof of a threat. Fear requires punishment and punishment requires bodies. The number of bodies that have been incarcerated at Gitmo is 770. For the first two years of the initial internment, the Bush administration asserted that the Geneva Conventions did not apply to the prisoners held on the base. A subsequent legal finding in 2006 overturned this claim, but the point of the extra juridical prison was clear. It was a place where no laws applied.

The Italian theorist Giorgio Agamben provides a framework for considering spaces like Guantanamo Bay. He calls them "states of exception": "The camp is the space that is opened when the state of exception begins to become the rule."⁵¹ He was interested in geographically produced spaces where the rule of law is temporarily disbanded, such as Auschwitz, Japanese internment camps in the United States, Native American reservations, or Guantanamo Bay. When considering the role of affect in the production of spaces of exception, I would argue that these spaces are the byproduct of widely circulated fear. When those in power successfully create a climate of fear around a certain group, they must create these states of exception to deal with the targets of that fear.

In considering the war on drugs, for example, Michele Alexander makes it clear that inner-city black communities fit the bill as states of exception. Their neighborhoods become places where incrementally constitutional rights are eroded to such a degree that the residents in these communities exist in a perpetual state of exception. It is not a ludicrous comparison between the conditions of a prison and the conditions in the actual neighborhoods where the residents have become synonymous with crime itself.

Much has been discussed regarding the rise of prison populations and the ill-conceived production of Gitmo. Barack Obama may have stridden into office with the intention of promising to close Guantanamo Bay, but at the end of his presidency, its existence remains. These infrastructures based on the continual use of fear produce a one-way-door scenario. One can use fear to build things, but one cannot use fear to unbuild them. The same is true for vast infrastructures of securing ranging from police to the military. The language to increase their importance and funding is easy to produce, but the rational discussion detailing expenditures, redundancies, and flawed creation just simply does not make for good headlines. To be fair, the news isn't the only culprit. Studies, articles, and reports detailing the fact that incarceration doesn't rehabilitate have been around for a long time. They just don't leave an impression in the mind of the public.

The prison system and Guantanamo Bay are just two

examples of a myriad of infrastructures resulting from the use of culture as an expedient for public attention and support. These infrastructures cannot be solely explained in terms of dollars and cents. They are fiscally untenable, and most politicians are well aware of that fact. But the knowledge at all levels of government is that being soft on crime or soft on terrorists is simply an untenable position (for now). Certainly, the United States, a country whose government spends $589 billion on the military while spending $72 billion on education and $26 billion on housing and urban development has an entire national budget that reflects this machination. The ground seems to be shifting in terms of the prisons and Guantanamo Bay, but the tools of cultural manipulation have the capacity to produce yet another enemy. New infrastructures of fear await, and old ones continue to be difficult to tear down.

RESISTING THE FEAR MACHINE

How do we resist the politics of fear? Even as history offers us a number of examples of alternative, antagonistic responses to the dominant culture, it can seem daunting to tackle something so large and sophisticated. In his book, *Dream: Re-imagining Progressive Politics in the Age of Fantasy*, New York University professor Stephen Duncombe suggests that progressives need to fight on the same terrain as the right by—to some extent—embracing the right's much-used deep-seated irrationality to stymie their goals: "Both fascism and commercialism share core characteristics of spectacle: looking beyond reason, rationality and self-evident truth and making use of story, myth, fantasy and imagination to further their respective agendas."[52] Duncombe suggests that progressive politics could use these skill sets to produce a sense of hope and a horizon of utopian possibility. By fully embracing the culture game, progressive politics might be able to use the power of narrative and storytelling to lure the imaginations of a broad public away from the cynical manipulations of the right wing: "Progressive dreams, to have any real political impact, need to become popular dreams. This will only happen if they resonate with the dreams that people already have—like those expressed in commercial culture today, and even those manifested through fascism in the past."[53]

Duncombe's plea does make a great deal of sense given what we've seen in the last few chapters: if culture is the province not only of advertising, but also of politics and the news media, then it seems foolish not to play the culture game. Still, we've also seen just how uniquely powerful fear really is—and how embedded its actual political consequences really are. (Never mind that mass media always prefers individual narratives to systemic analysis, making the mass movements' task that much harder.) In that sense, trying to fight fear with hope is a little like trying to open a lock with a wet noodle.

Yet there's a noble history of successful responses to the

politics of fear. In the late 1980s and early 1990s, AIDS activists were especially effective in interrogating and disrupting a language of fear that was then depressingly widespread within the unholy alliance of the Moral Majority, the political right, and its enablers in the media. Take the art collective Gran Fury, a spin-off of the AIDS activist group ACT UP. Gran Fury produced an advertising campaign that sought to recirculate images that provoked fear—and by doing so, sought to mitigate it. In 1989, the group circulated images of mixed-race and same-sex couples kissing with the words, "Kissing Doesn't Kill, Greed and Indifference Do," first on postcards, and eventually on the sides of buses. This was one of a number of visual strategies, all in service of a single goal: to conquer fear with humanity, to combat paranoia and homophobia by depicting images of love and compassion.

Success on one's own terms—as with Gran Fury—might be anomalous, but even if, as we saw above, well-orchestrated movements like Occupy Wall Street often can't remain telegenic for the reasons they want, anti-mainstream groups can use the overzealous nature of law enforcement to their own advantage. For example, the alt-globalization movement kicked off in response to the Seattle police's total overreaction to the anti–World Trade Organization (WTO) protests in November of 1999. The tear gas and the tanks proved effective in propagating awareness of a group of 40,000 protesters who would not have otherwise received major coverage for their skeptical attitude toward trade talks.

The sensational battle in the streets gripped the global news. And while even *The New York Times* fell prey to inaccuracy (the paper reported—incorrectly—that anarchists had thrown Molotov cocktails), the cameras continued rolling as pepper spray filled the streets for three days. The protestors chanted "The Whole World Is Watching," and they were right.

Over the next two years, protestors sought to meet the global ruling elite at any gathering they organized. And the nature of the protests evolved in a more media-savvy direction: movements like Carnival Against Capital turned protests into street parties; artist-activists went in playful directions, like Andrew Boyd, whose mock political group Billionaires for Bush got a great deal of attention; and irony ruled: in Spain, the art collective Las Agencias produced a fashion line for protests called *pret a revolter*. All of it was savvy and inventive and promising, and all of it ended on September 11, 2001, at which point the media spotlight honed on in a wholly different kind of antagonism.

I've already mentioned some of the successes and challenges faced by Occupy Wall Street, but it's worth looking at Occupy from another angle: the movement's fleeting but powerful conquest of the culture acutely reveals how much has changed since the alt-globalization era. Today's media environment isn't necessarily more favorable (it almost certainly isn't), but it's certainly more democratic. Social media has leveled the playing field in the culture wars in recent years, from the streets of Tunis to Zuccotti Park. After all, even though Occupy didn't endure as a national story, the protestors themselves had an unprecedented degree of control over their own mythmaking: one could now dictate the terms of protest from a smartphone, without waiting to see what the anchors in the studio thought.

It's fitting, then, to turn to one of our most promising contemporary protest movements, whose triumph is inseparable from the ascent of technologies that have helped spread its message. I'm speaking, of course, about Black Lives Matter, which began, appropriately enough, as a hashtag, following the acquittal of George Zimmerman for the murder of Trayvon Martin, and gained traction following the violent and high-profile deaths of a series of African Americans.

Initiated by three community organizers—Alicia Garza, Patrisse Cullors, and Opal Tometi—Black Lives Matter has become a major activist force over the last few years, and its ascent is inseparable from the growing power of social media. The criminalization of the black community has become impossible to ignore: the killing of black youth had made major headlines in large part because of Black Lives Matter's effective leveraging and circulation of video footage, most of it shot on smartphones. Police violence wasn't an unknown fact, but the combination of strategic activism and new technologies turned it into a national story. The results are still uncertain, but the impact of the visibility of the deaths of Eric Garner, Michael Brown, Tamir Rice, Freddie Gray, Sandra Bland, Laquan McDonald, and too many others—all of these events first revealed via smartphone or dashcam—may prove enormous. If television footage of Selma made the civil rights movement inescapable, all this footage may end up being equally historic.

And of course, it wasn't just the images themselves. Just think about their impact: everything from the protests in Baltimore, New York, and around the world to Beyoncé Knowles's iconic performance at the Super Bowl halftime show. The latter, though a considerably more constructed, stylized event than the former, shouldn't mean that it's unimportant: what we're watching, in real time, is the circulation of radicalism—the way that culture can move quickly, the way that fear can be repurposed. And all of it is so fast, so big, and so effective that it cannot be ignored by the very media organs who ignored the trends and perpetuated the very destructive politics that Black Lives Matter seeks to overturn.

Black Lives Matter and the associated activism has repurposed, but not eliminated, fear. On the contrary, like the alt-globalization and Occupy protests before them, the protests against black violence have provoked a great deal of anxiety and fear—much of it racist, and thus far more intense than anything we saw in 1999 or 2011. This activism has unleashed the very fear it meant to counteract.

This contradiction, though, shouldn't make us question the efficacy of protest, or the wisdom of trying to reappropriate and repurpose culture; if anything, the contradiction only makes the need for more activism on the cultural level more urgent.

5

THE REAL ESTATE SHOW

It was inevitable: the book, the author, the whole kit and caboodle. Richard Florida's *The Rise of the Creative Class* was published in 2002, a moment of profound ennui for cities across the country. The dot-com bubble had burst, as had its promise of endless high-wage jobs for the techy youth of America. But Florida offered an alternative—a siren call that transfixed government officials, city boosters, and anyone invested in urban success.

Florida spoke of a new kind of city that would attract a new kind of worker. Manufacturing plants were gone and weren't coming back, but out of the ashes of steel mills, automobile plants, and textile factories would arise the soy-milk lattes, artisanal-cheese shops, web-based advertising agencies, and spin classes of the new global, urban age. Skilled workers would trade in their ties for Celtic armband tattoos and move to cities where they felt comfortable, stimulated, and well-fed. And real-estate brokers would follow, finding crash pads for the best and brightest.

Born in Newark in 1957, the son of a Depression-era factory worker who had made his way up the chain, Richard Florida was the quintessential contemporary cultural figure. He may not have thought of himself as an artist, but his impact has—undoubtedly—been cultural. His model of urban revitalization has weathered intense criticism from all sides, and though his legacy is ambiguous at best, his writings and even his personality have played a central role in shaping attitudes toward the role that culture should play in the city—and the decisions that emerge as a result of those attitudes. If physics has an observation effect, by which observing a physical phenomenon alters it, Florida demonstrated what we might call the urban-physical effect: he may have begun in a purely observational role, but through his conferences, institutes, books, and nonstop charisma, he actively transformed the American city.

Florida's tone was optimistic—hypnotically so. He wanted a better planet. He wanted to overthrow the staid, unimaginative bureaucrat in favor of individualism, ingenuity, innovation, development, and ultimately, prosperity. He spoke without equivocation, painting a picture of a city rich with diversity, tolerance, and technology. He was perfect for the TED stage: a big-picture thinker who eschewed negativity and difficult subjects like class, race, and gender. Why get into all that when everything came down to design—and to worldview? Cities didn't need to redress imbalances of power or inequity: they simply needed to catch the wave of the information economy.

What Florida understood in 2002—and what makes him a central protagonist of this book—was the role that culture would play in the reshaping of the twenty-first century metropolis. Culture wasn't, he argued, something to be locked away in art galleries, museums, performing-arts centers, or movie theaters. Instead, it was an integral element of the new city. Culture could be a tool, a piece of infrastructure, not unlike roads or street lights or office parks or school districts.

Florida's insights weren't especially groundbreaking in and of themselves. Academics such as Manuel Castells, David Harvey, and Saskia Sassen have long argued that the post-Ford age and the rise of the "information economy" would lead to a major urban restructuring: cities would grow much bigger, more influential, and more central to the world's economic life. Vast urbanization became a crucial area of study for cultural geographers, urbanists, global theorists, and economists. Florida's unique contribution to this discourse could be described as more vaudevillian. Unlike the planners and historians who carefully laid the groundwork for his claims, he opted for grandstanding and panache. He was a showman—more P. T. Barnum or Ronald Reagan than Harvey or Sassen. His books were readable, exciting, and optimistic, and they lacked any of the fussy contradictions that so often make theoretical books . . . well, difficult. He was tan. He was fit. He spoke in an authoritative, conversational style that made everyone in his jam-packed conferences feel good. He talked about the future, about diversity, about making the world a better place, and he did it all with an appealing lack of specificity. For Florida, everything was a win-win.

Florida wasn't and isn't wrong—at least, not exactly. The picture he painted of the contemporary global city has made it much easier for people to interpret the changes that have occurred in their own towns—and in many cities worldwide. His prophesies were quite accurate: the economic composition of the United States' new global cities after the collapse of manufacturing really does resemble what he described in *Rise of the Creative Class*. Florida took up the mantle of livable-city theorists like Jane Jacobs and William Whyte, but he was less concerned with observation and analysis and more concerned with outcomes. He foregrounded the kinds of neighborhood conditions that would attract the people he called "creatives," a new economic class he essentially invented—a class unrelated to income that could enfold everyone from knowledge workers to artists to designers to computer programmers to engineers to scientists. And creatives needed somewhere to live.

Developers embraced Florida's terminology—they were now appealing to creatives—and added their own. The first waves of post-Ford urban dwellers weren't merely new residents looking for deals: like Americans who set out for the West a century and a half earlier, the new gentry were "urban pioneers" who had discovered this new land called the city.

Florida drew chart after chart to reveal how the creative class had contributed to unparalleled financial growth in cities ranging from the greater Silicon Valley, to Boulder, to Austin, to Portland, Oregon, to New York City. The numbers didn't lie, and cities that didn't appear in the charts started paying attention. Florida emphasized over and over again that the creative class was different from new urban populations of the past. To cater to them, cities needed diversity and coffee shops, arts and tolerance. Florida made it look easy: attract the hipsters, and Google would follow.[54]

The rise of this new class and of creativity as an economic force were the underlying factors powering so many of the seemingly unrelated and epiphenomenal trends we had been witnessing, from the ascent of new industries and businesses to changes in the way we live and work, extending even into the rhythms, patterns, desires, and expectations that structure our daily lives.

Mayors across the country heard the call. They began to devote more and more of their limited city resources to attracting the creative class. It was time for an image change: their cities couldn't merely provide jobs and space and resources—they were an image, a brand, a lifestyle. Even cities that hadn't been gutted by the collapse of manufacturing couldn't afford to rest on their laurels: to succeed on Florida's terms, they had to change their very culture.

BRANDING THE CITY

In their pamphlet *Branding Your City*, a group called CEOs for Cities explains that in an age of vast global competition, cities have to sell themselves:

> Put simply, branding is a tool that can be used by cities to define themselves and attract positive attention in the midst of an international information glut. Unfortunately, there is the common misconception that branding is simply a communications strategy, a tagline, visual identity or logo. It is much, much more. It is a strategic process for developing a long-term vision for a place that is relevant and compelling to key audiences. Ultimately, it influences and shapes positive perceptions of a place.[55]

When it was published, *The Rise of the Creative Class* tapped into city planners' and government officials' nascent anxieties about how to make their cities relevant in the twenty-first century. If Florida were right that cities would have to reshape themselves to attract throngs of the creatives, then those cities would have to advertise themselves. But this was only the beginning. As CEOs for Cities shows, the work of creativization would take much more than a logo. Every new innovation—every new form of urban living—would be part of the sales pitch and be the sales pitch itself: a bike path wouldn't be only a bike path, but also an opportunity to promote a cool, livable city to businesses looking to make a change. The city itself would become a living, breathing brand.

Over the last thirty years—and especially in the Richard Florida era—the logic of advertising transformed the American city. As cities began to compete ever more aggressively for investment, residents, and tourism, they experienced an increasingly familiar pattern of revitalization. The techniques have varied to some degree, but there is plenty of continuity. Think of the major architectural projects designed by so-called starchitects like Gehry, Koolhas, Diller and Scofidio, Calatrava, and Hadid. As time goes on, even the most accomplished of these big, looming, futuristic buildings seem less like functional solutions to urban problems, and more like beacons to capital. All those wiggles and twists and funny shapes can, after all, get your city noticed.

A predecessor to the contemporary phenomenon known as *placemaking*, the Guggenheim Bilbao remains the most perfectly emblematic example of the starchitectural model of urban development. In 1991, Thomas Krens, director of the Guggenheim Museum, was approached by Basque city officials who were desperate to revitalize the moribund port city of Bilabo. In their quest to transform Bilbao into a tourist destination, they offered to cover the cost of the construction and manage the museum after it was built. Krens saw the opportunity as a way to fulfill his dreams of international expansion: he wanted to franchise his renowned cultural institution.

Frank Gehry's architectural creation was unprecedented, truly one of a kind. With twisting titanium shapes that brought to mind a gilded slice of lasagna or an elegant sailor's knot, the museum gleamed and hovered like a spaceship over the sleepy seaside town. And as promised, the tourists came. In just the first three years, the museum had exceeded the most optimistic expectations for tourist revenue and visitors and was paying for itself. Gehry, Krens, and Bilbao had caught the world's imagination. Here then, was the formula for making a splash on the global stage. Culture, it seemed, could literally make a city come to life. The city could become a thriving brand.

From museums, to cows: in 1998, one could hear *mooing* along Michigan Avenue in Chicago. That year, Peter Hanig, the president of the Greater North Michigan Avenue Association, paired up with Lois Weisberg of the department of cultural affairs to bring to Chicago a simple public-art initiative conceived in Zurich the previous year. The idea: Cows on Parade.

Cows on Parade set into motion a pattern of numerous global initiatives that aimed to integrate culture into urban life. Half city branding, half half-baked, Cows on Parade were a series of manufactured fiberglass cows painted and decorated by local artists and displayed in front of numerous businesses and civic locations. At the end of their tourist-friendly run, the cows were then auctioned off, with proceeds donated to a charity.

People Magazine described the bovine cultural phenomenon in 1999:

The creatures, including a likeness of Mrs. O'Leary's cow (rumored to have started the 1871 Chicago fire), "are loved to death," says Mike Lash, director of the Chicago Public Art Program. They have also generated mucho moo-la: some $100 million in tourism revenue. After Oct. 31 the cows will be auctioned for charity, not put out to pasture. Says Hanig: "We're gonna milk this for all it's worth."[56]

And milk it they did. The cows became an international urban-planning sensation. Through the combined vision and efforts of business and city government, Michigan Avenue was transformed into a fun, family-friendly playground of artistically driven, wacky cow creations. There were cows painted like zebras, American flag cows, Van Gogh cows, and even the Cowpuccino, sponsored by Starbucks. Local artists finally had a way to participate in the visual culture of major shopping districts, and revenue poured in. With over a million tourist visitors, the Cows on Parade became a model for artistic city collaborations and spread to metropolises everywhere. From their humble beginnings in Zurich and their breakthrough in Chicago, the cows morphed into city-specific canvas for the world's many economically precarious, socially alienated artists. Now artists could take part in the marketability of the new creative city, which would inevitably end up displacing them. There were lions in Leipzig and Jerusalem, shoes in Istanbul, cats in the Catskills, salmon in Salem, guitars in Austin, dragons in South Wales, and on and on—each iteration a new, viral icon.

One could call the cows a vast public-art experiment, but above all they were a geography-specific form of urban branding, and their introduction into the landscape of Chicago was part of an overarching strategy to change Chicago's image. No longer would it be the city of gangsters, of industry, of "Big Shoulders." The Chicago of the twenty-first century was an arts-friendly metropolis. In this sense, the cows went hand in hand with the city's new Millennium Park, with its iconic Anish Kapoor Jelly Bean and a bandshell designed by Gehry. The city of Chicago—the home of Leo Burnett, Saul Alinsky, Jane Addams, and the Haymarket martyrs—was now a proper, contemporary brand, with its own Gehry, its own Kapoor, and its own cows.

CORPORATE BOHEMIA

And as cities worked harder and harder to refine their brands, actual brands were light years ahead in sophistication. Advertising in the 1990s honed in on the figure of the rebel. Our most iconic cultural figures—Mahatma Gandhi, Martin Luther King, Jr.—were untethered from the movements they led and the histories they evoked: they now stood in for cool companies, like Apple. Che Guevara was reincarnated as the Taco Bell Chihuahua, and Jack Kerouac was no longer a classic or overhyped writer (depending on one's perspective): he was a posthumous pitch-man for the San Francisco–based retailer Gap.

But if the 1990s was the era of the rebel in advertising, the first decade of the twenty-first century brought about a further evolution. What advertising had done in 1990s was sell the image of bohemia to consumers increasingly alienated from the concept. But one could do more than allude to bohemia to sell clothes, tacos, and computers—one could *produce* it.

In the 2000s, Starbucks coffee became nearly synonymous with revitalization efforts in cities. What could be more emblematic of the rise of the new urban renewal—urban renewal on Richard Florida's terms—than the towering figure of Starbucks? For city dwellers, the Frappuccino house's ruthless exploitation of predatory pricing and real-estate politics was a powerful lesson that showed just how effective a corporate-driven bohemia could be. The green siren logo was thus much more than a clever piece of branding: it was a warning shot—a strong implication that a neighborhood was about to become corporatized and unaffordable.

Of course, Starbucks merely exploited an ongoing tendency. In a contemporary metropolis focused on the creative class, the arts (and everything the term connoted) were a perfect partner for investment. It isn't as if the bohemias of old functioned entirely outside of capital, but the distance between Charles Baudelaire stumbling around Paris and the mural of Baudelaire in San Francisco's posh North Beach neighborhood is tremendous.

What has happened over the last twenty years might be called the commodification of bohemia, but ultimately, that's too weak a term to describe the tendency. Because what has taken place in Berlin's Kreuzberg, in the Mission District in San Francisco, in the Mississippi neighborhood in Portland, Oregon, and in Williamsburg, Brooklyn, adheres to a specific formula (of course, there are oh so many more neighborhoods out there as well). These neighborhoods and cities were "hipsterized" according to a repetitive logic. As people began to move back to cities, big business and local governments worked to attract the horde by any means possible. This meant less casual, contingent, anarchic bohemias, and more prefabricated versions thereof that could be sold seamlessly.

BLOWBACK

In the 1950s, the Central Intelligence Agency coined the term *blowback* to describe the unintended consequences of a covert operation. The Contras, Al Qaeda, and even ISIS: blowback. The blowback that occurred in American arts funding looks something like this: the National Endowment for the Arts and its bevy of like-minded philanthropists used the Floridian language of revitalization to sell the arts, but somewhere along the way, they began to use the language of arts to sell revitalization. The consequences were unintended, and unideal.

In the 1990s, the National Endowments were still reeling from the culture wars of the late 1980s, and their chairs did everything they could to learn the lessons of their past. They saw the arts as too concentrated in New York City, and thus began to support more institutions across the whole country—the South and the Midwest started to get money as well. They stopped handing out grants directly to artists and chose instead to use institutions as buffers, so that if endowment money funded a performance artist who, say, got naked, the link wouldn't be quite so direct. These were careful and cautious organizations, struggling to find a place for the arts in the twenty-first century.

No one could have been more helpful in their effort than Richard Florida himself. Florida's preferred terms—revitalization and diversity—became the new battle cry for NEA chair Rocco Landsman. Just after two months in his tenure, Landsman was confronted with a renewed effort to draw the NEA back into the culture wars of the 1980s. Attempting to shore up their base with conservative values, Republicans initiated a familiar fight with the Obama administration, this time over a David Wojnarowicz video at the National Portrait Gallery that dared to devote a few seconds of its running time to a crucifix crawling with ants. So he took a new tack: "We don't want to spend hours responding to attacks on us by whomever," he told the *Los Angeles Times*. "We want to go out and talk about arts education and the arts as it relates to the economy—we're going to be aggressive."[57]

What a difference twenty years made. The National Endowment for the Arts finally had their hands on an argument that could diffuse familiar—and damaging—xenophobic, homophobic, and sexist attacks. Rather than defending an artwork based on freedom of expression, or as a good in and of itself, the government could shift the conversation toward the productive role the arts play in the economy.

Even the graphs and charts that accompanied Florida's argument seemed to have found their way into the foundations' work. It was clear that the arts were no longer distinct from their commercial counterparts, such as advertising, radio, television, and software—art, too, could be a useful part of the creative economy. The 2012 Otis College of Art Report on the Creative Economy is representative of the new tendency: it contains a revealing chart that shows that visual arts and performing arts workers make, on average, $204,772. That kind of number is enough to make any curatorial assistant, dancer, painter, performance artist, or art handler blush, which is why you have to read the fine print: it turns out that the category includes Hollywood actors and screenwriters. The inclusion of this community makes the chart feel slightly misleading, but it's telling: if one is eager to prove that the arts do, in fact, assist the economy, then surely one must include the most robust parts of the arts economy in one's calculations.

This reunification of the arts with their commercial counterparts would not have surprised Adorno and Horkheimer. As we've seen, for the two theorists, culture was *always* a business and an industry. And now the NEA agreed. The illusion of a healthy creative economy was more important than actually diagnosing the health of a community using culture to do things other than make money. A visual artist's average pay couldn't help but tell a sad story about that economy, but if you included the salaries of web developers, programmers, and advertising designers, the contribution to the local economies would look much more attractive. This form of statistical tweaking was born out of desperation, and those who lobbied on behalf of the arts found it difficult to resist.

Desperate to find an argument for its very existence, the NEA shifted its motto from "Because a great nation deserves great art" to "Art works." The model would no longer be focused on excellence based on taste, but rather on the way that culture could *make things happen*. The arts were now an engine—a machine in the new city. They had aligned themselves with the one indicator that politicians could understand: capitalism. Pundits, planners, and re-energized granting agencies could now use sophisticated metrics to assess the cultural vibrancy of everywhere and everything: that art "worked" was a testable proposition.

Art worked, and it would work on behalf of economic development. Chicago's cows and Austin's guitars didn't have to be great—they merely had to stimulate development and contribute to "vitality." Creative Cities International (CCI), an organization very much of its time, developed a vitality index to assess what they describe as a "good messiness at the top. "As they put it:

> The vitality of a creative city distinguishes it from just any urban environment. The exemplar creative city is

full of energy, opportunities and interesting people combined with a bit of edginess. That creative tension, which
is the result of an entrepreneurial spirit combined with
restless talent wanting the city to be more remarkable or
provide better outlets for ideas and energy equals what
we call "good messiness."[58]

As some of the aforementioned examples—Portland,
Brooklyn, Kreuzberg—have shown, "good messiness" rarely
works out in practice. In these places, and many more cities
suffering from the loss of manufacturing jobs, the wage cap
between those working at good salaries for information
economies and those stuck behind were palatable at every
level. Often also breaking down in terms of race, the promise of the creative city did not take into account the growing disparity in wealth and the effects of displacement that
would soon consume many urban centers. Florida himself
has acknowledged this, as has Lisa Lees, CCI's director.
"Can the VI be used for purposes of branding and marketing cities?" Lees asked in a 2011 interview. "Certainly.
Crucially, however, what we feel best attracts tourists, new
business, and young people is what the city is already doing
for the people who live there—the 'inner tourist.'"[59]

But benefitting long-term residents is much easier said
than done. If the deployment of culture toward specific,
developmental, economic ends over the last twenty years
have shown anything, it's that Lees's "inner tourists" rarely
benefit en masse. Many urban dwellers have been pleased
by the regeneration and hipsterization of their cities, but

more often than not, they were likely to reap the benefits regardless of developmental patterns. Who, after all, is the creative economy for? And who benefits from measures like the vitality index? Florida is worth quoting at length on this topic:

> Gentrification is by no means a black and white issue. Back in 2002 when I asked Jane Jacobs about this, she explained that gentrification is more a gray area. While she was appalled at the "generica-fication" of Soho and other urban neighborhoods, she used her own neighborhood of the Annex [in Toronto], close to the university, as an example of "good gentrification." Sure, new coffee shops, chi-chi shops, and upscale restaurants had moved in, but there were still local hardware stores, pubs, ethnic restaurants, and mom-and-pop shops. New residents with more income were restoring old buildings and making the neighborhood stronger. But there was a tipping point, she explained. When I pressed her on the social costs brought on by displacement she looked up at me and explained that neighborhoods and cities go through a dynamic process of development. "When a place gets boring," she said, "even the rich people leave."[60]

Sameness, then, is a larger concern than economic equality. Per Jacobs, in diversifying amenities and not falling prey to corporatization, one can stave off the purgatory that is the blandness of corporate culture. But how to actually redress the inequalities that emerge when outcome-driven arts foundations, boosterish city governments, and creative-economy advocates compete for a city, many of whose "inner tourists" have little stake in its development? The answer remains elusive, and the actual commitment to solving the issues remains lukewarm at best. Indeed, somewhere along the line, analysis got confused with prescription. Rewarded with handsome speaking fees, Richard Florida succeeded at transforming global economic trends into a practical economic language that people could see and feel. The cities were changing. Everyone could see that. Everyone was talking about it. But then what?

The city is an advertisement, and culture is a crucial component of our economic life. These two facts are key to understanding why contemporary cities look and feel the way they do, and what exactly many arts granters, urban economists, city planners, and government officials worldwide have been up to. Starchitecture, cows on parade, and vitality indexes: these are the weapons of our new culture industry. That industry has had enormous impact on downtowns and fringe neighborhoods, on old factory buildings and new arts districts. And it has made real-estate speculators and developers rich.

AN INSURRECTION

The intention of this action is to show that artists are willing and able to place themselves and their

work squarely in a context which shows solidarity
with oppressed people, a recognition that mercan-
tile and institutional structures oppress and dis-
tort artists' lives and works, and a recognition that
artists, living and working in depressed communities, are compradors in the revaluation of property
and the "whitening" of neighborhoods.
—REAL ESTATE SHOW MANIFESTO

The story goes something like this: artists move into an
affordable part of the city. More often than not, this neighborhood, like other low-income neighborhoods in other
cities, is ethnically diverse, with small mom-and-pop stores.
More economically mobile people begin to move in—generally middle class, but not always: the cheap rent is a lure,
but they might also find the diverse environment to their
liking. The new residents have more cash to expend, and
they begin to develop galleries, record stores, coffee shops,
bars, and so on. The neighborhood becomes more affluent,
and as it attracts more and more people with increasingly
higher levels of income, rents and property values increase.
Eventually, these economic transformations of the neighborhood efface the very ethnic diversity and affordability
that made the area attractive in the first place, along with
the low-income renters and owners (and artists) who made
it their home. This is, of course, the process ubiquitously
known as gentrification.

Gentrification is the dark shadow cast over even the
most appealing neo-bohemias, and the most innocuous

forms of hipsterism. As Richard Lloyd writes in his book
Neo-Bohemia, which examines the gentrification of Chicago's Wicker Park neighborhood, "Rather than looking
at artists as a resistant subculture, I became compelled to
think of artists as useful labor, and to ask how their efforts
are harnessed on behalf of interests they often sincerely
profess to despise."[61] For Lloyd, and frankly many urban
denizens at this point, the correlation between art gallery
and new development became nearly synonymous.

As we've seen, for pundits like Richard Florida, ambi-
guities notwithstanding, the role that culture can play in
the production of the new, successful, modern city is always
a net gain. And yet the fight against gentrification that activists, artists, enlightened politicians, neighborhood associations, and ordinary residents have waged for decades
is fundamentally an attempt to relitigate this story. People
have watched with wonder and horror as their neighborhood and cities have been transformed in front of their
eyes, usually with none of their input. It's never been an
easy fight, but their resistance is a crucial motif in the story
of the cultural conquest of cities in the United States and
around the world.

One of the consequences of the wars against gentrification has been an increasing mistrust toward the idea of culture itself. How can culture be a universal social good—or
even neutral—when so much upheaval has been unleashed
on its behalf? In many cases, culture has become a dirty
word. Capital, after all, has had a long tradition of rear-
ranging space to suit its own ends, and while the conse-

quences of gentrification have been far milder than those of, say, the urban renewal of Robert Moses's highway construction, one cannot fault anyone inclined toward historic corollaries. Florida is far from unaware of urban history—of the racial oppression and the devaluing of land inherent in these stories—yet too often, he has helped replicate its worst patterns. Perhaps he and the city boosters believe that it's in capitalism's interest to promote a more tolerant society. But there are plenty of reasons to be skeptical of this conclusion.

Despite the efforts of historians and journalists (including, recently, Ta-Nehisi Coates's major intervention in the pages of *The Atlantic*), the story of redlining and discriminatory-housing practices has never quite sunk into the American consciousness. In the 1930s, the National Housing Act and the Federal Home Loan Bank Board's maps based on neighborhoods' racial composition enshrined segregation for generations. Communities of color were unable to purchase their homes, and over time, they suffered greater and greater inequities when it came to homeownership, the United States' most solid form of savings.

The impact of gentrification is of course not as extreme, nor as intentional in its design, but the result is distressingly similar. In her 1998 book *Evictions*, Rosalyn Deutsche writes, "When galleries and artists, assuming the role of the proverbial 'shock troops' of gentrification, moved into inexpensive storefronts and apartments, they aided the mechanisms by driving up rents and displacing residents."[62]

Those mechanisms, as we've seen, were an old story, but the impact of culture made them new. Deutsche's analysis was self-evidently true in 1998; nearly twenty years later, it has become an inescapable fact of life, even for city dwellers who have never met an artist.

Like the history of redlining, gentrification is also not a story that's well understood. It manifests itself more clearly in the public consciousness, yes, but solutions on the level of policy—local, state, or federal—tend to be minimal to nonexistent. The transformation of American cities has thus been a kind of secret war—discussed at length, but very rarely acted on.

Rarely, but not never. Two days before the end of the 1970s, a handful of artists broke into an abandoned factory showroom in the Lower East Side of New York City. They used bolt cutters. They pasted the windows. They swept up the trash and made themselves at home. It was a break in, and they knew it. The squatted exhibition that opened two days later, titled *The Real Estate Show*, came together out of a deep sense of frustration regarding the radical transformation of the neighborhood. As the artist Alan Moore wrote at the time, "A lot of people are tired of getting the short end of the stick in the real-estate world because of forces they don't understand but that always amount to money."[63]

The Real Estate Show was one of the earliest antigentrification projects, and its lessons, language, and concerns seem downright prescient today. The exhibition opened on New Year's Day, accompanied by a party along Delancey Street. The following day, the artists showed up to find the building padlocked. As Lehmann Weichselbaum wrote in 1980, "*The Real Estate Show* had been open exactly one day. Its basic ideological premise—that artists, working people, and the poor are systematically screwed out of decent places to exist in—could not have been brought home with more brutal irony."[64]

Negotiations with the police department followed, and the altercation between artists and a city that refused to let them use New York's many vacant and abandoned buildings garnered increasing attention in the community press. To galvanize broader interest, the artists went uptown and lured the visiting German artist Joseph Beuys down to the site. With Beuys in tow, the artists held a press conference in front of the still-closed doors, as uncomfortable-looking cops stood by. Police removed the artworks in a surprise raid, but ultimately, the artists were offered an alternative space located at 156 Rivington Street. They acquiesced, and 156 Rivington went on to become the primary hub for punk-rock shows, anarchist organizing, and the occasional art exhibition.

This story sounds familiar enough, except the part where the police brokered a deal. Back in 1980, the city of New York owned a number of vacant properties whose market value was nearly nil to hand over and compromise with, which today is clearly no longer the case. Inner-city property is now a hot commodity. But the concerns that the artists voiced then are the concerns that one continues to hear today. In the film *My Brooklyn*, MIT professor Craig Wilder says, "The process of gentrifying Brooklyn

is not necessarily making Brooklyn a better place to live.
The process of gentrification in New York is not about
people moving into a neighborhood and other people
moving out of a neighborhood. The process of gentrification is about corporations sectioning off large chunks of
those neighborhoods and then planning out their long-
term development."[65]

The paradigmatic example of contemporary resistance
to gentrification is none other than Bill Talen, better
known as the Reverend Billy. Reverend Billy is a one-man
anti-Starbucks narrative—a man without fear who jumps
into the spotlight with the alacrity of a Warhol neophyte.
He loves the press, and he loves the truth. He is up against
corporate culture and its commitment to sameness, which
he fights with every ounce of his being. Reverend Billy's
crusades began in Times Square, which was subjected to
an onslaught of corporatization in the early nineties. He
was a preacher that didn't mind the sex but hated the consumerism. Waving a stuffed Mickey Mouse over his head,
he preached a gospel opposed to shopping: "We will remove Starbucks and Disney! Make them close their doors!
We'll do our shopping in an owner-run business! We won't
go back, no more!" From the Disney Store, he moved on
to other corporate targets. He got himself a motley crew
of Lower East Side denizens turned anticorporate gospel
singers called the Stop Shopping Choir. He invaded corporate chain stores, transforming them into temporary
public-art spaces. He gave wailing speeches with tremendous eloquence and fever. He perspired. He raved. Over-

throwing the money changers, he led a crusade for the people against corporate culture, ridiculing them for their myopic greed and exploitation. His speeches were moving. They tapped into a feeling shared by many New Yorkers that the city was selling its soul.

The good reverend was against not only sameness, but also the obsessive consumerism that dominated contemporary urban life, and even more than that, the growing hubris that accompanied corporate demands on public life and space. By stepping squarely into a corporate lobby (as opposed to using the few public spaces left), Reverend Billy was making a claim that every physical space was a place for potential dis-census, another term for democracy. It was a place to disagree.

And there was so much to disagree with. It seemed that no matter what any activist, community organizer, or tenant association attempted, developers' desire to "clean up" the city proved victorious. And everyone knew what they meant by cleaning up: attracting business and cultural development, and delivering a swift kick to the poor.

Fortunately, the backlash continues to echo. In 1998, the anarchist-inspired Biotic Baking Brigade caught the then mayor of San Francisco Willie Brown squarely in the face with tins of pie cream. He was announcing a clean-up campaign of Hunts Point/Bayview, and to this particular group of miscreant pie-flingers, his collusion with developers necessitated a good pie-ing. And in 2010, crowds that had gathered for a first-Friday event in the Tophane neighborhood of the Beyoglu area of Istanbul—where numerous galleries had set up shop—were assaulted by a mob of angry antigentrification activists. There are hundreds of stories like these.

In Austin, Texas, residents have wrestled with the difficulties of creative-class "success." In 2000, Austinite DJ Red Wassenich coined the phrase "Keep Austin Weird" as a euphemism for the deep desire shared by numerous residents that the city was losing its charm due to rapid development. Perhaps one of the more glaring examples of Florida's creative-class predictions, the city launched into the spotlight as a haven for musicians, artists, and technology firms. The massive music festival South by Southwest exploded in sales and performers, and it now ranks as the largest music festival in the world. The growth of cultural options accompanied equal growth in real-estate development. Home prices in parts of Austin have more than doubled, and the growth through the city has been fast and furious.

Which meant, of course, that the city was growing more and more unaffordable for the artists and musicians who made it a "creative" space. With a perverse irony, "Keep Austin Weird" evolved from the gripe of a proud town to a pro-local business slogan to an effective branding campaign for the city. The originator of the phrase lost a court battle that would have prevented the phrase from being copyrighted by a company called Outhouse Designs. Now the phrase adorns tourist T-shirts, bumper stickers, and key chains—the perfect accessory for thousands of music fans and curiosity seekers hoping to glean whatever it is that was so worthy as to make the phrase come into existence.

CULTURE WARS IN THE CITY

As cities are replanned, rezoned, and rebuilt, culture is increasingly used as a developer's battering ram, and artists worldwide are having to assess what their relationship is to the things they make—and the ways they live. This, then, is a different kind of culture war. It's a war for the right to the city that has, over the last few decades, developed a strong cultural inflection. If in the past the methods for uprooting people and keeping them from their homes was blunter and harsher, now the means are more subtle, more cheerful, and culturally inflected. There are fewer major demolition projects and far more cows, gleaming buildings, and coffee shops. Yet the players remain powerful and influential—grant-giving organizations with massive clout, real-estate developers who are happy to rebrand as long as they attain their desired outcomes, starchitects eager to serve the highest bidders, and the pundits that spin the whole story into something uplifting and inspiring.

One doesn't have to be Richard Florida, or the global theorist Manuel Castells, or a grant-making organization eager to rebrand, or Reverend Billy, or an antigentrification activist in Istanbul to see the central role that culture plays in the very production of urban living. As we've seen, Art Works. It works brilliantly well, and in many crucial ways it's not all that different from a bulldozer or a cement mixer. But if on its own terms, the selling of art and culture has been wildly successful for its stakeholders, the question of whom it's actually served—and whom it hasn't—remains hauntingly ambiguous.

Fortunately, artists are more aware than ever of their own role in this process, and so are activists and residents, but then again, so are the antagonists—politicians, developers, foundations, etc.—who are finding ever more refined ways to speak the language of cultural development. Who will win? Perhaps that's a premature question. But many questions must be asked urgently, and loudly, if cities can have a chance to belong to the people who build them.

6

THE INSURGENTS

Community-Based Practice
as Military Methodology

It is inevitable that the story of the culture war in America would involve the military, specifically the military invading the terrain of that thing we call *culture*. And while I don't pretend that any causal connection exists between the world of the military and the world of nonviolent, community-based artistic practice, comparing the two can tell us much about the weaponization of culture.

Comparing the military and the arts certainly reveals a difference scale. In the United States, the former enjoys a national-funding budget of $683 billion and the other ekes by on $706 million (and that's the *entirety* of all arts funding in the United States, and the funding for community-based art practices would be a mere fraction of that). Operationally, one group kills and at times tortures people while the other, at worst, coopts injustices for aesthetic or careerist reasons. Structurally, one group of people follows a vast hierarchical chain of command, making the cog-in-a-machine analogy a good thing, whereas the other privileges the space of the autonomous individual, and even when working collectively the numbers rarely exceed four or five. But in both counterinsurgency and community-based organization, people become involved for the basic reason that also has attracted people to anything from marketing teams to religious groups: getting to know people is the only way to change the social landscape, and thus to alter power dynamics. The same fundamental social project is behind getting to know people as an occupying force, or getting to know people as neighbors.

So far I have discussed real-estate gurus like Richard Florida and marketing giants like Starbucks, but the story of the military's uses of culture takes on a darker tone. I am not going to focus on the military's use of propaganda, nor their attempts to rebrand themselves. I am not even going to go into the mid-twentieth-century attempts to use abstract expressionist painting to demonstrate American values of freedom to the world. Instead, we have much to learn from the military's active interest in cultural approaches to counterinsurgency.

HEARTS AND MINDS

By the fall of 2005, the Iraq War had hardened into a political and military quagmire. But as a man who had often quoted the mantra, "If you have a problem and you can't solve it, make it bigger," Secretary of Defense Donald Rumsfeld continued to exacerbate the problem of the Iraq War. U.S. casualties remained relatively low—2,170 dead and 15,955 wounded—but the Iraqi death toll was estimated at a brutal 30,000, and anything that could be called progress by President Bush and his media team appeared elusive.[66]

Two years earlier, Bush had stepped off the USS *Abraham Lincoln* aircraft carrier with a fluttering "Mission Accomplished" banner waving behind him. Now, the war had reached proportions that reminded many Americans of the ignominious police action in Vietnam. The Iraq War had been a sham to begin with (a manipulation of the United States' post-9/11 fears; a cultural war in and of itself) but the thinking at the State Department was that a quick victory abroad would heal domestic wounds. Donald Rumsfeld, Ambassador Paul Bremer, and General Tommy Franks had unleashed their strategy of shock and awe: pummel the enemy so heavily that they would simply give up the will to resist. But after two years, no one could exactly point to who the enemy was or how to stop them. After two years, the military needed a new and more nuanced plan.

That plan was hatched in Fort Leavenworth, Kansas, where then lieutenant general David Petraeus called upon an array of fellow West Point thinkers to rewrite a forgotten military document: the counterinsurgency Field Manual 3-24. In his book, *The Insurgents*, military historian Fred

Kaplan makes the convincing case that the writing of the field manuel itself was an internal act of insurgency (a revolution in the way the military thought about insurgents). The field manual resisted the gun-toting shock and awe–style methods that had dominated military doctrine since the Vietnam War, emphasizing instead the value of protecting the people better and conquering their social landscape faster than the enemy. Petraeus understood the value of "getting to know people," because their feelings and attitudes toward the direction of a conflict would greatly influence its outcome. As Mao Tse-tung is often aphorized, "People are the sea that revolution swims in."

The preface to Field Manual 3-24 states, "Counterinsurgency is military, paramilitary, political, economic, psychological, and civic actions taken by a government to defeat insurgency."[67] The handbook is perhaps the most informative guide to a military strategy, emphasizing the transforming of popular perception as a supplement to straightforward killing. One needs to replace knocking *in* doors with knocking *on* doors to avoid producing scores of more insurgents with every belligerent act.

Petraeus's rewriting of the book marks the cultural turn in the U.S. military. That's right, the military had its own cultural turn.

FM 3-24 is fascinating. It is not only a companion to some of the great books on war, including Carl von Clausewitz's *On War*, Sun Tzu's *The Art of War*, Mao Tse-tung's *On Protracted War*, and David Galula's *Counterinsurgency Warfare*, but it is also interdisciplinary like the best books on the uses of culture, including Antonio Gramsci, Saul Alinsky, and Paolo Freire. If one can detach one's ethical allergy to books on violence, one would be surprised by the technologies of culture outlined, the dizzying account of skill sets applicable to marketing, retail outlets, war, and art alike. Above all, it is a book on how to shape public perception. "The primary struggle in an internal war is to mobilize people in a struggle for political control and legitimacy."[68] The production of a legitimate state, in essence, depends on changing the attitudes of the people in a country. And in teasing through the techniques, a set of skills that takes seriously the role of culture becomes visible.

In a section titled, *Ideology and Narrative*, the field manual states, "The central mechanism through which ideologies are expressed and absorbed is the narrative. A narrative is an organizational scheme expressed in story form. Narratives are central to representing identity, particularly the collective identity of religious sects, ethnic groupings, and tribal elements." Narrative, here, is a two-way street. It is the medium through which people process their perceptions. It is also the medium through which they define themselves to the rest of the world. And it is manipulatable in both directions: in this case it can be influenced to enhance the perception of U.S. military presence as a positive thing, and influenced to spread that idea. Increasingly in the twenty-first century, narrative is a means of self-articulation and expression of worldview manipulated by marketers, PR consultants, and the military alike.

The lessons of cultural postmodernity had at last been

codified into military thinking. And while the notion that "American ideas of what is 'normal' or 'rational' are not universal" seems obvious, one should not overstate the complexity of this cultural turn in the U.S. military. The military is a vast machine. Having a field manual on counterinsurgency updated to reflect basics in contemporary anthropology and lessons ranging from the Philippines to Algeria to Vietnam does not mean that eighteen-year-old soldiers on the ground suddenly become masters of cross-cultural relationships. Quite the opposite. As much as Petraeus and his crew of counterinsurgency gurus understood that culture was a necessary battlefield in warfare, they did not know how to effectively enact such changes in the world's largest bureaucracy.

Emblematic of this shortcoming is the Iraq Culture Smart Card created in 2003. A sixteen-page laminated cultural cheat sheet, this guide was produced to give a quick lesson to soldiers making their way through the war-torn streets of Iraq to facilitate their cultural knowledge. The card reads like a pamphlet on the rules of poker, but it is a guide for war. It offers mini-lessons on history, Islamic religious terms, female dress, and gestures. As Rochelle Davis writes about the smart card, "To be sure, this example of cultural knowledge (factually incorrect as it may be) says more about the U.S. military and its conception of culture than it does about Iraqis or Arabs."[69] Indeed, it says much about the state of the U.S. military that 1.8 million were initially manufactured in 2003 and that they continue to be distributed.

The creation of Field Manual 3-24 and the Iraq Culture Smart Card epitomized a push toward a new way of understanding war, a new style of hearts and minds campaign. Since at least the Vietnam War, the military has been long overdue for a shift in personality and culture. The cultural turn was not only an emphasis on understanding the culture of the other, but also the internal transformation of the culture of the military itself. It was chicken soup for the military soul.

PEACHES: THE MAYOR OF MOSUL

Born in Cornwall on Hudson, New York, to Miriam and Sixtus Petraeus in 1952, David Patraeus graduated in the top 5 percent of his 1974 West Point class, going on to eventually lead military operations in Iraq, Afghanistan, and then the Central Intelligence Agency. Petraeus is also referred to by friends as "Peaches." An avid jogger, a survivor of a bullet wound to the chest, a survivor, again, from an accidental fall from a parachute, and reported to be as hardworking as he is ambitious, David Petraeus is a military man through and through.

In 2003, Major General David Petraeus, commander of the Army's 101st Airborne Division, was fifty years old and in charge in Mosul, Iraq. In the wake of Bush's declaration of victory, it became immediately clear that something has gone terribly wrong. When Paul Bremer fired the ruling Ba'ath Party members from public-sector jobs, the occupation of Iraq took on an even uglier composition as an insurgency rose up overnight.

Mosul was said to be the exception. It hosted press conferences and congressional visits, because word had gotten out that, unlike the rest of Iraq, progress was being made in this northwestern city. Using phrases like "money is ammunition,"[70] Petraeus had instituted some basic counterinsurgency methods to develop the local economy and build up a local Iraqi security force. He ordered his 7,000 troops walk instead of drive through the city. Foot traffic seemed to provide an interpersonal connection to the local residents. "We walk, and walking has a quality of its own," states Petraeus. "We're like cops on the beat."[71]

An insightful comment indeed. Perhaps Baudelaire and Petraeus could ruminate on their shared admiration for walking. Not that COIN-trained soldiers in Mosul are necessarily flaneurs, but they do, in a sense, drift. They drift through the ruins of a city with makeshift lean-tos, congested traffic, cinder-block buildings, fruit stands and booksellers with their wares on wooden pallets. The soldiers knock on doors, get to know people, and become in a sense a face with a name. Simultaneously, so the Mosul residents are becoming people to the soldiers. As Walter Benjamin writes of the flaneur, "He . . . enjoys the incomparable privilege of being himself and someone else as he sees fit. Like a roving soul in search of a body, he enters another person whenever he wishes." A neat image for the friendly occupier.

Petraeus held local elections, began road reconstruction, and reopened factories. As Joe Klein wrote in *Time* magazine, "He was, in effect, the mayor of Mosul."[72] Patreaus spent as much time fixing the economy as he did finding insurgents. He arranged an agreement between local sheiks and Iraqi custom officials for trade with Syria. According to *The New York Times*, "Three months later, there is a steady stream of cross-border traffic, and the modest fees that the division set for entering Iraq—$10 per car, $20 per truck—have raised revenue for expanded customs forces and other projects in the region."[73] The stunt in Mosul worked for Petraeus.

Petraeus's efforts in Mosul succeeded in garnering the attention of the higher-ups at their wit's end as what to do with the war. Having written his Ph.D. thesis from Princeton on "The American Military and the Lessons from Vietnam: A Study of American Influence and the Use of Force in the Post-Vietnam Era," Petraeus was obsessed with the operational lessons of the Vietnam War, as well as the mental scars it had produced in the military chain of command. Shock and awe wasn't just a military strategy of dominance, but a direct result of a military culture that refused to get themselves involved in the protracted ugliness that was another occupation. *Never again* was the operating logic. Petraeus had studied the uses of counterinsurgency on an occupied force, but he also intuitively understood how to manipulate the internal mechanisms of war culture to further his agenda (and thus his career).

Petraeus was nominated to the head of central command of Iraq, which solidified what is described as the "cultural turn" in the military. The overarching switch in emphasis that makes COIN (military shorthand for *counterinsurgency*) so different from other military strategies is its emphasis on people and culture. After World War II, in conflicts such as in Vietnam, El Salvador, Nicaragua, and Panama, wars reflected colonialist projects more than the "nation-state at war" model. In these colonialist-type projects, COIN operations became increasingly useful, as they emphasize the restructuring of political and economic conditions to gain the support of a disempowered public. In a paradoxical sense, COIN operations often reflect the values of the very left-wing movements that they have historically opposed. But a tool is a tool.

FIGHTING THE LEFT BY BEING THE LEFT

General David Petraeus's strategies in Mosul came out of a combination of research and firsthand experience. Although the Iraq War was his first time in combat, he had traveled to El Salvador in 1985 with General Jack Galvin to see up close what a counterinsurgency campaign looked like. The United States under Carter and Reagan was determined to stop the spread of left-wing governments worldwide, fearing Cuban and Soviet interference in both El Salvador and Nicaragua. In El Salvador, they sent in military "trainers" (they eschewed the term "advisors" due to its negative association with the Vietnam War) and weapons ($5 billion in aid total) to support the right-wing government that was decimating the revolutionary movement of the Farabundo Martí National Liberation Front (FMLN). The U.S. trainers facilitated a conflict that came to be regarded universally as a human-rights nightmare. One million people were displaced and, according to the United Nations, 75,000 thousand people were killed in a nation of roughly 5.5 million. In State Department circles, however, the conflict in El Salvador was viewed as somewhat of a success, since the leftist FMLN never came to power.

The U.S. generals and trainers behind the counterinsurgency in El Salvador had to engage in perverse doublespeak, since the right-wing government they were supporting not only lacked legitimacy in the eyes of El Salvadorians, but also in the eyes of the U.S. military. According to Fred Kaplan, Brigadier General Fred Woerner, who headed up the military strategy team in El Salvador, "drafted a National Campaign Plan that addressed what he called 'the root causes' of the insurgency. It laid out a program of rural land reform, urban jobs, humanitarian assistance, and basic services for a wider segment of the population."[74] Ironically, these policies were precisely the kind that the rebels were fighting for, which the right wing never would have established.

In essence, the U.S. trainers and other military personnel in El Salvador were seeking the same thing as their left-wing enemy. As a 1991 RAND paper aptly summarized:

In El Salvador, as in Vietnam, our help has been welcome but our advice spurned, and for very good reason. That advice—to reform radically—threatens to alter fundamentally the position and prerogatives of those in power. The United States, with its "revolutionary" means of combatting insurgency, is threatening the very things its ally is fighting to defend. Those reforms that we have deemed absolutely essential—respect for human rights, a judicial system that applies to all members of Salvadoran society, radical land redistribution—are measures no government in El Salvador has been able to achieve because they require fundamental changes in the country's authoritarian culture, economic structure and political practices.[75]

With the lessons he learned in El Salvador in mind, Petraeus replaced General George Casey as commanding general in Iraq in 2007. During his confirmation hearings, Petraeus articulated his idea for "the surge," which he saw as his opportunity to put into practice everything he had laid out in *Counterinsurgency*, Field Manual 3-24.[76] The U.S. military would firm up the new Iraqi government, provide safety for its citizens, separate the extremists from the moderates, and bolster local police forces. He also brought in several advisors who had long supported the growth of culturally inflected COIN thinking within the U.S. military, including an Australian lieutenant colonel named David Kilcullen. Kilcullen had written a widely circulated document titled "Twenty-Eight Articles," which condensed the lessons of counterinsurgency into a how-to guide for soldiers. Petraeus asked Kilcullen to again write up a simple list explaining COIN strategy to soldiers involved in the surge. Understanding the occupied population and offering them security were crucial.[77]

The result was a militarized campaign of "getting to know people." The surge didn't produce immediate results, and over the first few months, casualties among U.S. soldiers actually spiked (due in large part to their greater presence on the ground). But after the first half of 2007, civilian and troop casualties declined dramatically.

With the perceived success in Iraq, Petraeus emerged as a miracle worker. In the eyes of administration officials, he had taken an impossible situation and somehow turned it around. On April 23, 2008, President Bush nominated Petraeus to run U.S. Central Command (USCENT-COM), located in Tampa Bay, Florida. Two years later, on June 23, 2010, President Obama nominated Petraeus to replace General Stanley McChrystal as the head of the International Security Assistance Force in Afghanistan—the thinking being that if COIN could work in Iraq, maybe it could work in Afghanistan as well. Petraeus's kinder, gentler form of warfare also seemed to fit perfectly with the public image of President Obama, whose 2008 campaign was targeted to voters fed up with the bellicose blundering of George W. Bush.

The most important influence on David Petraeus's counterinsurgency thinking was a French military strategist named David Galula, who many regard as the historic expert on counterinsurgency. His 1964 book, *Counterinsur-*

gency Warfare: Theory and Practice, languished in relative ob-
scurity until the U.S. military rediscovered COIN in the
early 2000s. Galula lived one of those peculiar lives marked
by consistently being in the center of historic events. A
French citizen born in Tunisia in 1919 and raised in Casa-
blanca, he graduated from the prestigious Saint-Cyr military academy in 1939. In 1941, he was expelled from the
officer corps under the Vichy government's ban on Jews.
He relocated to North Africa. There he joined the French
Resistance during World War II, and then rejoined the
French military. In 1945, he was deployed to China, where
he witnessed firsthand the Communist revolution headed
by Mao Tse-tung, who was battling the Kuomintang na-
tionalists. Galula wound up being captured and held for a
week. In captivity, he began to notice that Mao was fighting a very different kind of war. As Adam Curtis[78] writes:

> Put simply—there was no conventional army any longer,
> the new army were the millions of people the insurgents
> moved among. And there were no conventional victories
> any longer, victory instead was inside the heads of the
> millions of individuals that the insurgents lived among.
> If they could persuade the people to believe in their cause
> and to help them—then the conventional forces would
> always be surrounded—and would be defeated no matter
> how many traditional battles they won.[79]

In 1956, Galula volunteered to fight in the Algerian
War. He wanted to test out a series of ideas he had been

formulating on counterinsurgency. He deployed them in a mountain village, where he hoped to talk the revolutionaries into changing their minds:

> In March 1957, I was well in control of the entire population. The census was completed and kept up to date, my soldiers knew every individual in their townships, and my rules concerning movements and visits were obeyed with very few violations. My authority was unchallenged. Any suggestion I made was promptly taken as an order and executed. Boys and girls regularly went to school, moving without protection in spite of the threats and terrorist actions against Moslem children going to French schools. Every field was cultivated. As they recognized the difference between their prospering environment and those surrounding areas still in the grip of hostilities, villagers were easily convinced of the need to preserve their peace by helping to prevent rebel infiltration.[80]

Counterinsurgency is a method—a method of talking to and coercing people. If you take away the use of violence (which is like taking the flour out of a cake), COIN bears a remarkable similarity to that left-wing, walking-the-beat technique known as grassroots organizing. In the current landscape of everyday life—whether in Baghdad or in Oakland—culture, the built environment, politics, and media are all inextricably intertwined.

COMMUNITY ORGANIZATION AS NONVIOLENT INSURGENCY

The strategy of getting to know people is employed by all kinds of activist groups, from grassroots organizations, to church organizations (the Mormons and Jehovah's Witnesses know a thing or two about going door to door), to community-based artists, NGOs, and civic organizations. While it's unlikely that very many of these do-gooder groups have studied the writings of David Galula, they have probably been influenced by the writings of Saul Alinsky.

Born in 1909 to Russian Jewish immigrants in Chicago, Alinsky, like so many others, became radicalized during the lean years of the Great Depression. He organized in the predominantly Slavic neighborhood known as Back of the Yards, made famous by Upton Sinclair's *The Jungle*. A dirty mess of meat-packing plants, the working conditions there were the kind of grave injustice that fueled Alinsky's visionary pragmatism. He was a realist and refused allegiance to any ideology. His efforts became the foundation for what has become contemporary community organizing.

Not at all unlike the community-building strategies described in *Counterinsurgency*, Field Manual 3-24 or in the writings of David Galula, Alinsky's community-organizing methodology relied heavily on the creation of a network of councils whose combined interests resulted in real political power. Here are the thirteen principles of community organizing, from his seminal book *Rules for Radicals*:

- Power is not only what you have but what the enemy thinks you have.
- Never go outside the experience of your people.
- Whenever possible, go outside the experience of the enemy.
- Make the enemy live up to their own book of rules.
- Ridicule is man's most potent weapon.
- A good tactic is one that your people enjoy.
- A tactic that drags on too long becomes a drag.
- Keep the pressure on.
- The threat is usually more terrifying than the thing itself.
- The major premise for tactics is the development of operations that will maintain a constant pressure upon the opposition.
- If you push a negative hard and deep enough it will break through into its counterside.
- The price of a successful attack is a constructive alternative.
- Pick the target, freeze it, personalize it, and polarize it.[81]

Alinsky's rules for radicals come out of a deep understanding of how to manipulate public perception in an uneven playing field. In essence, Alinsky's rules describe how to organize a *nonviolent insurgency*, which is one way to characterize community organizing and socially engaged art. Perhaps it is no wonder then that the current organizing methods of the Tea Party have been credited to Alinsky's sage examples.

While Petraeus didn't exactly organize community meetings to improve labor standards, as he took over the war in Afghanistan he was primed to organize meetings with tribal leaders. His credibility after Iraq was at an all-time high, and the Obama administration was eager to claim victory in the country where the Soviet Union famously failed. With support increasing in the White House for Petraeus's hearts-and-minds strategy, so too did the budget for more advisors, translators, social programs, and payoffs. One of the most talked about and controversial of these programs was called the Human Terrain System (HTS).

HUMAN TERRAIN

The Human Terrain System launched in February 2007 as the brainchild of the U.S. Army Training and Doctrine Command (TRADOC). The project's peculiar name reveals plenty about the its aspirations. Just as the military needs to understand the topography of the countries it invades, it must also map the complexity of the population.

> According to its website, "The Human Terrain System develops, trains, and integrates a social science based research and analysis capability to support operationally relevant decision-making, to develop a knowledge base, and to enable sociocultural understanding across the operational environment."[82]

With an initial budget of $20 million, HTS funded five teams in Iraq and Afghanistan. These Human Terrain Teams (HTTs) included translators and anthropologists and were intended to gather intelligence by meeting face to face with community leaders and support U.S. military operations.

HTS met with almost immediate controversy, especially in the halls of left-leaning academia. In November 2007, the Executive Board of the American Anthropological Association issued a formal rebuke of the HTS's militarization of the discipline:

> In the context of a war that is widely recognized as a denial of human rights and based on faulty intelligence and undemocratic principles, the Executive Board sees the HTS project as a problematic application of anthropological expertise, most specifically on ethical grounds. We have grave concerns about the involvement of anthropological knowledge and skill in the HTS project. The Executive Board views the HTS project as an unacceptable application of anthropological expertise.[83]

However strong the condemnation from anthropology's most distinguished body, some anthropologists still participated in HTS. Certain academics who normally would never find themselves at the center of military culture were suddenly thrust into the limelight, as the desperation for new solutions on the part of the U.S. military forced atypical cross-disciplinary relationships to emerge.

Such was the fate of the enigmatic figure Montgomery McFate.

In 2005, Montgomery "Mitzy" McFate cowrote, with Andrea Jackson, a short piece titled "An Organizational Solution to DOD's Cultural Knowledge Needs," which argued for the creation of a new department to consolidate cultural information during a war effort: "Establishing an office for operational cultural knowledge would solve many of the problems surrounding the effective, expedient use of adversary cultural knowledge."[84] The timing was perfect, as interest in a cultural method of COIN was growing among the military brass. McFate, perhaps knowingly, cleared a path for a future department in which she would play an important role.

Holding a Ph.D. in anthropology from Yale and a law degree from Harvard, Montgomery McFate took an unlikely route to the inner sanctum of the Department of Defense (DOD). In the same year that she published the article on the DOD, she also published an odd article titled "Anthropology and Counterinsurgency: The Strange Story of their Curious Relationship." Here McFate made a series of zigzagging rhetorical maneuvers to demonstrate that anthropology's fear of replicating colonialism had forced anthropology to run from any kind of political relevance— such as cooperation with the U.S. military:

> The retreat to the Ivory Tower is also a product of the deep isolationist tendencies within the discipline. Following the Vietnam War, it was fashionable among

anthropologists to reject the discipline's historic ties to colonialism . . . Rejecting anthropology's status as the handmaiden of colonialism, anthropologists refused to "collaborate" with the powerful, instead vying to represent the interests of indigenous peoples engaged in neocolonial struggles.[85]

Most of the academic community and many in the broader media saw McFate's arguments as a rationalization of her newfound position of power, but McFate, who wasn't afraid to challenge the hermetic nature of academia, argued that helping the military could lead to saving lives. "If you understand how to frustrate or satisfy the population's interests to get them to support your side in a counterinsurgency, you don't need to kill as many of them. And you certainly will create fewer enemies."[86] It is a brutal logic, hard for many to stomach.

One of her most vociferous detractors, Hugh Gusterson, wrote, "The anthropologist turned military consultant Montgomery McFate . . . (and others) are suggesting a form of hit-man anthropology where anthropologists, working on contract to organizations that often care nothing for the welfare of our anthropological subjects, prostitute their craft by deliberately earning the trust of our subjects with the intent of betraying it." It wasn't necessarily inaccurate, but McFate had already become a darling of the cultural turn in COIN.

LIFE: AN EXTENDED PERFORMANCE

What COIN initiatives like the Human Terrain System attempt to accomplish is something that the artists, marketers, and politicians are all trying to achieve. The premise is that social relationships have a medium and can be given a form. The cultural turn in the military over the last thirty years has been counterbalanced with a cultural turn in contemporary art and community organizing.

In 1993, black youth in Oakland had a public-image problem. The war on drugs was in full effect, and the mainstream media had portrayed them as a pathologically violent class of people. Enter the artist Suzanne Lacy, who had been volunteering in Oakland public high schools teaching classes on media literacy. She organized a series of conversations with teachers and students—not unlike something Alinsky would organize. Some of the students were interested in having their voices heard in the media, a realm from which they were usually locked out. Working with Lacy, they produced an event they hoped will allow them back in. The performance, titled *The Roof Is on Fire*, features 220 high-school students sitting in parked police cars on a roof talking about their lives. The situation was purposefully odd. A rooftop as a place for conversations in cars would be strange enough, but black youth having public conversations with police was altogether unheard of. And perhaps what made the encounter all the more surreal yet urgent was the obvious fact that these two groups probably have the most to talk about. The performance was part media stunt, part community organizing effort, part art project.

Suzanne Lacy studied under artist Allen Kaprow at the University of California at San Diego. Kaprow is historically known for experimenting with this type of blurring of the line between art and life: "The line between the Happening and daily life should be kept as fluid, and perhaps indistinct, as possible."[87] Lacy took this to mean that life itself could be choreographed and shaped. Public encounters could be used as clay by an artist. When Lacey was studying under Kaprow in the mid-'70s, the second-wave feminism that would inform her work was taking hold in the arts, especially on the West Coast. Thus, the influence of Kaprow and the political period of the time came to inform a practice that would define socially engaged art to come: a political art practice that worked with people in public to produce unique, and dynamic, encounters.

In 1977, Lacy created the project *Three Weeks in May,* which focused on violence against women. She described it as an "extended performance" occurring over three weeks. The project unfolded in a series of life-like activities that mimicked the techniques of a community-organizing campaign. Speeches by politicians, press events, radio interviews, art performances, and self-defense workshops were all choreographed movements in this theater of political life.

Lacey built upon the work of Kaprow by tackling political issues—by bringing art not only into daily life, but also into political and social life. She addressed the contextual realities of power. This focus places her work in conversation with other discourses that have attempted to shape everyday life—that regard people as the center of gravity. Lacey and the likes of David Galula, Saul Alinsky, and David Petraeus employ community-organizing techniques to mold the "human terrain."

IT ISN'T EASY

Easier said than done. Changing public attitudes is no mean feat, particularly when you are an invading, colonizing force. With the perceived success of the surge in Iraq, the United States refocused on Afghanistan, with an even larger emphasis on the role of Human Terrain Teams. The fit was less than ideal. Poorly trained anthropologists trying to blend in with and give advice to highly trained soldiers came with its own culture clash. According to retired colonel Steve Fondacaro, who headed up the Human Terrain System program in Afghanistan, "We're like a germ in the body of [the Army] . . . All of their systems are sending white blood cells to puke me up."[88]

The United States is not a monolithic machine. It is a cumbersome infrastructure with competing, if not outright, conflicting interests. As much as the stated desire to protect and study the population were part of the mandate of HTTs and the overarching COIN operations in general, these operations often found themselves overshadowed by the vast brutality that is the legacy of U.S. military conquest.

Recruiting for the HTTs wasn't easy—thanks in part to the academic backlash against McFate—even with the fairly large paycheck that was offered. Initially, the ideal candidate spoke Arabic and had a Ph.D. in anthropology with a focus on the Middle East. But the qualifications were quickly relaxed to include anyone with a graduate degree in anthropology, and soon enough, anyone with a graduate degree in almost any related field. As one might imagine, having a graduate degree in sociology doesn't exactly prepare one for learning about the intricacies of Pashtun tribal culture in the midst of a war. Journalist Robert Young Pelton followed an HTT around Afghanistan and learned just how odd the fit was:

> HTTs are supposed to bring down the cultural barrier between the military and the locals, but the biggest enemy is the natural inclination of troops to be troops, not social workers. Strangely enough, the Taliban is far more expert at meeting the basic needs of Afghans: namely, by fighting the corrupt central government and providing justice and security. Until that changes, the Afghans will be more inclined to identify with the "enemy" than the well-intentioned guests.[89]

A bad fit in a war zone can come with gruesome results. On November 4, 2008, thirty-six-year-old HTT member Paula Loyd was conducting routine surveys in a village in Kandahar Province. She had graduated from Wellesley with a degree in anthropology and had spent years as a development worker in the region. But all her training did not prepare her for the man she was interviewing to suddenly douse her in gasoline and set her on fire. She died from her burns a few months later. Her attacker, Abdul Salam, was shot while in custody by Loyd's HTT colleague Don Ayala. Ayala was put on trial and found innocent.

Of course war is violent and the death of one HTT member isn't exactly a condemnation of the program. But that narrative took hold in the media. A blond-haired do-gooder being set on fire didn't sit well with the news-watching public and produced a backlash of skepticism regarding the effectiveness of the Human Terrain System program.

On May 2, 2011, at 11:35 p.m. EST, President Obama announced that U.S. troops had raided a compound in Pakistan and killed Osama bin Laden. It was perhaps the first time a U.S. president could claim an unqualified victory in a 9/11-related military expedition. It was enough to put the brakes on COIN operations in Afghanistan—which were steadily losing support. On June 22, 2011, President Obama announced by the end of the year, 10,000 troops would be withdrawn from Afghanistan, and that by the end of 2012, 35,000 more would be withdrawn. Then on June 30, 2011, David Petraeus was confirmed as the director of the Central Intelligence Agency. He left his post in Afghanistan. The priorities of the U.S. military had radically shifted.

From there the story takes a tabloid-esque turn. Steve Fondacaro had already been let go in June 2010 as the military already began having second thoughts about the potential success of the Human Terrain System program. Then it was discovered that Montgomery McFate, writing under the pseudonym "Pentagon Diva," was the person behind the entertainingly titled blog *I LUV A MAN IN UNIFORM*. The blog gushed over the hotness of the commanders of the wars in Afghanistan and Iraq. The last post, written on June 15, 2008, reads, "Why is Dave Kilcullen so totally, spankingly HOT? Is it because he's an Australian Army officer with a Ph.D. in anthropology and operational experience in multiple theaters? Is it because he gives full body contact hugs? Is it because he was instrumental in Petraeus' surge strategy in Iraq?"[90] This discovery was likely a contributing factor in McFate's dismissal from the Human Terrain System program in August 2010.

The tabloid story doesn't end there. Famously, Petraeus was outed as having an extramarital affair with his biographer, Paula Broadwell. The affair came to light after Tampa Bay socialite Jill Kelley, a friend of Petraeus, received threatening e-mails regarding her friendship with the general. She turned the e-mails over to the FBI. The internet trail eventually led back to Broadwell. The scandal culminated in the resignation of Petraeus. It also took down General Paul Allen, who had inherited Petraeus's position in Afghanistan. E-mails between himself and Jill Kelley came to light, and although Allen was cleared of any wrongdoing, he stepped down a few months later. Petraeus may have come into the war as the mayor of Mosul, but by the time he was ousted from office, he was persona non grata and his cultural turn a failure.

MEANS AND THE END

We must learn from power even if we do not agree with it, especially if its tactics embroil us in a protracted and ultimately failed war. Petraeus's Field Manual 3-24, I believe, holds many valuable truths about manipulation that must be taken into account.

I am not in the least bit equipped to argue whether McFate's premise that COIN would save lives is accurate. Nor can I say what kind of timetable and financing Petraeus would have to possess in order to achieve what he would deem a success in Afghanistan. I do, however, believe that the implementation of COIN points to both the power of community organizing and offers useful insights into the thinking of those that pair social power with violence.

As much as Walter Lippmann, Ivy Lee, Richard Florida, and Ingvar Kamprad were all enthusiasts and practitioners of the uses of culture, none of them positioned such a practice in direct conversation with violence. Edward Bernays is the exception in his consulting for the United Fruit Company in Guatemala in the 1950s and their U.S.-backed counterinsurgency efforts. Nevertheless, pairing violence with an on-the-ground strategy of community building not only has clear historic precedents, but also tells us much about the techniques of cultural manipulation at the disposal of power. For it is one thing to talk about the convincing power of narrative or the methods by which once can seduce a viewer through desire, but quite another to talk about telling people a story they should believe or die. Such is the high-stakes game of the military, but frankly, such is the high-stakes game of living in a political world.

It might seem counterintuitive to compare the arts and the military, but while the ends pursued by these two spheres are radically different, aspects of their means are startlingly similar. Comparing their means of narrative shaping offers a new method for understanding formal approaches to the construction of public opinion. As the manipulation of culture becomes a priority across a range of disciplines, it is necessary to look beyond disciplinary boundaries and simply compare methodologies.

The cultural turn in the military was no small initiative. It reshaped the war in Iraq and put thousands of troops on the ground in Afghanistan. While its urgency has waned for the moment, the interest in military force operating on the level of culture will only grow as wars increasingly take place in urban environments, a web of cultural relations and the territory of all cultural actors, be they artists, police officers, marketers, or pedagogues. The different ends may or may not justify the means, but the means themselves teach us much about competing uses of culture.

7

SOUNDING THE TRUMPET

Charity and the Image of Doing Good

On October 29, 1929, the bottom fell out of the U.S. stock market. A stark contrast with the golden era of the roaring twenties, the Great Depression took the average American on a tour of the poorhouse. Beggars all. By 1932, 25 percent of the American workforce was unemployed and hungry. The burden of this massive systemic failure overwhelmed the U.S. government, and the charities and churches came to the rescue. Soup, that economical wet meal that dates back to 20,000 BC, would be paired with bread to keep Americans on their feet. Soup kitchens were born.

With poverty now commonplace, soup lines extended through the downtowns of all major cities. Men in overcoats and fedoras lined up to acquire their daily nourishment. Even the American gangster Al Capone boasted of feeding 120,000 with his very own soup kitchen.

Soup, poverty, and charity have been bedfellows for a

long time. In Calcutta, India, 1949, Mother Teresa made a name for herself offering soup to those whom she called, "the poorest of the poor." Famously, she took a vow of poverty, and with that vow came a lifelong connection to soup. She took her cue, of course, from the words and deeds of Jesus himself who espoused care and sympathy for those in need.

And before Mother Teresa, in 1210 Saint Francis of Assisi, inspired by Jesus's adoration of the meek, took a vow of poverty and initiated what would become a vast infrastructure of Catholic charity known as the Franciscan order.

Soup and charity. Charity and soup. It isn't just a metaphor. It is a meal. Seven hundred and fifty-two years after St. Francis, thirty years after Black Tuesday, and a mere thirteen years after Mother Teresa began her quest to fill the mouths of the needy, a young Andy Warhol took his fondness for soup to the canvas. Thirty-two silkscreened varieties of Campbell's soup, including chicken with white rice, vegetable bean, tomato, black bean, and split pea, went on display at Irving Blum's Ferus Gallery in Los Angeles. A series of red, white, and black clans with comforting familiarity, these images of grocery-store consumer products would eventually take the nation by storm. They earned Warhol celebrity status and launched the age of pop art.

While Warhol's Campbell's soup cans have become so iconic as to perhaps rival the ubiquity of Campbell's soup cans themselves, his focus on the United States' working-class meal is the subject here. It is said that Warhol loved soup. In his own words, Warhol explained, "I used to drink it. I used to have the same lunch every day, for twenty years."

A boy from steel-town Pittsburgh, and son of Carpatho-Rusyn immigrants, he had been fed a daily dose of Campbell's soup for most of his life. He was truly a child of the Great Depression.

To say Warhol was intuitive is putting it mildly. Pittsburgh gave birth to an oracle; a beacon of American emotional undercurrents. Warhol understood exactly what had made Campbell's such a pioneer of the arcana of consumer products. Being the premier manufacturer of canned soup, Campbell's (established as the Joseph Campbell Preserve Company in 1869) paved the way for the mass manufacturing of cheap preserved foods. In 1897, the company developed a formula for commercially condensing soups, thus making distribution possible. But as we've learned, it's one thing to have an innovative product, and another to *look* innovative. The imagery of Campbell's, based on red, black, and white became iconic. And in 1899, the company headed full on into a new emerging field called mass advertising.[91]

The move to mass advertising increased their sales by 100 percent in one year, a lesson that would never be lost on corporate America. Images of the iconic can and color scheme became present in advertisements in newspapers and magazines. By 1931, Campbell's began to sponsor radio programs like the George Burns and Gracie Allen Show and Amos and Andy. By 1936, the company had become the eleventh largest advertiser on radio. In 1938, after Orson Welles's famous war of the worlds hoax on radio, Campbell's soup bought the program that hosted it, *The Mercury Theatre on the Air*, renaming it *The Campbell Playhouse*.[92]

Campbell's soup was not just a soup, it was an image that attached itself to the cultural vehicles of America.

Timing might be everything, and the Great Depression created the perfect moment for Campbell's soup. Able to sit on the shelf for over a year, these cheap cans of sustenance became a central part of daily life for a generation. Warhol was not alone with his twenty years of soup memories. It was ingrained in the United States' collective consciousness. And thus, with a stark red, black, and white image, the Campbell's soup can not only evoked the taste of tomato and chicken noodle, but also nostalgia and intimacy.

When Warhol presented this work in the gallery, he was, in essence, showing the beauty and peculiarity of tangled relationships which collided in a single packaged good. It was an advertisement. It was nostalgia. It was a product. It was food. And, going back to the work of Mother Teresa and St. Francis of Assisi, it was charity.

Fast forward to today. Every October, an eye-popping wash of pink swathes products and televised events in the United States. It is breast cancer awareness month, and for reasons perhaps tied to the enthusiasm and opportunities available in an age where the desire to do good can also be big business, the color pink has become a season unto itself. NFL jerseys and cleats go pink, joggers turn pink, M&Ms turn pink, bras go pink, and the Campbell's soup can, like a chameleon, drops its iconic color scheme to adopt the ultimate color of charity, pink.

"For the past twenty-five years, Susan G. Komen for the

Cure has been on a mission to end breast cancer forever," said Katrina McGhee, vice president of marketing for Susan G. Komen for the Cure. "Cause-related marketing programs such as Campbell's pink can program are an integral part of that mission, helping us reach millions of consumers with life-saving breast health messages and providing funds that support breast cancer research and community outreach programs."[93]

Campbell's soup initiated its breast cancer awareness campaign in 2006. The simple idea comes from the strategy that McGhee describes: cause-related marketing. In the first year, Campbell's soup donated $250,000 spread across three nonprofit women's philanthropies: Susan G. Komen for the Cure, Breastcancer.org, and Giving Hope a Hand, The Kroger Co.'s corporate women's health initiative. (The Kroger Co. is the second-largest grocery retailer under Walmart and also happens to be a major distributor of Campbell's soup.) Help out a cause while also helping out a friend who is helping out a cause. The pink campaign, in every way, was meant as a win-win. Help fight breast cancer and increase sales.

For the month of October, Campbell's soup doubled the distribution of their top sellers: tomato and chicken noodle—temporarily made pink. They even replaced their gold-medal medallion with the breast-cancer-pink ribbon. An overhaul of a look in limited edition. The sale of the cans themselves was not closely connected to the actual gift. The financial contribution was separate from sales, and when totaled after all was said and done, only 3.5 cents per can actually went to the donation. "We certainly think there is the possibility of greater sales since our typical soup consumers are women, and breast cancer is a cause they're concerned about," states Campbell's spokesman John Falkner.[94] Without irony, Campbell's sees its connection to breast-cancer awareness as a brand choice to reach out to women consumers. The charity, to be simple, is secondary in the extreme.

Breast-cancer cause marketing: it is the kind of movement that would make Edward Bernays proud. In a 2004 survey by the brand-strategy firm Cone, 91 percent of 1,033 consumers say they have a more positive image of a company or product when it supports a cause and 90 percent will consider switching to another company if it's aligned with a cause.[95] Certainly this has not been lost on the brands that go pink. As a cause that speaks to women, it is a moment for any brand trying to reach the women consumer. And most brands are.

If Warhol's soup made visible the associations between the homely, the nostalgic, the mass-marketed, and the mass-produced, the pink soup can multiplied the effect. And thus it becomes clear: the very deep human desire to help, and our positive associations with those that help, reveal much about the growing strategies of marketing and art as they dovetail with benevolent charity. Unpacking the ethics and implications of these maneuvers is no easy task. What is being sold? Is this charity? Is this capitalist entrepreneurship? Without trying to evade the issue, one has to admit that in the age of mass marketing and mass philanthropy, the space between doing good and the benefits of saying one is doing good is razor thin.

But before we interrogate the multibillion-dollar industry that relates in one way or another to charity, let us turn to one last story of soup. The lessons of soup are not just those of the bare-facts gift of giving, they are not just the image of charity, but soup poetically enough has a role to play in the arts and in particular as a medium whose very nature embodies the very human desire for exchange.

On April 1, 2011, a rickety windmill appeared on the roof of a once abandoned building in Philadelphia. Located on Girard Avenue, across the street from a public sculpture of Don Quixote, the windmill churned at the urging of the spring wind. Three stories down on the first floor, a sign adorned the exterior of the building with the simple words, "SOIL KITCHEN." Inside, one could see a workshop of sorts, with diagrams on a chalkboard, pamphlets on soil remediation, and soil samples hanging in the window, and in the air was the very familiar smell of home-cooked soup.

The one-week project was initiated by the Bay area–based artists Futurefarmers and supported by the city of Philadelphia with the assistance of Theresa Rose. The concept was simple: offer soup in exchange for soil samples. As a project that partnered with the Environmental Protection Agency, Soil Kitchen would test soil samples for contaminants. The exchange of soup became the foundation for a multifaceted project involving workshops, environmental assistance, and convivial sociality. The windmill was more than just a functional on the roof. In Futurefarmers' own words:

Rather than being "adversarial giants" as they were in the novel, the windmill at Soil Kitchen is a functioning symbol of self-reliance and literally breathing new life into a formerly abandoned building. The windmill also serves as a sculptural invitation to imagine a potential green energy future and to participate in the material exchange of soil for soup—literally taking matters into one's own hands.[96]

Three hundred bowls of soup were handed out daily made from two different vegetarian recipes with locally grown ingredients. Yes, it was a little crunchy in its adoration for locally sourced food, but the soup emphasized an atmosphere of sharing. You didn't even need to bring soil samples to get a bowl. You could just go up to the counter and get it. But this spirit of generosity, and also, the meal of soup, provided an atmosphere that spoke, and smelled, of an alternative to one dominated by capital and consumption.

The classes available in the Soil Kitchen also presented alternatives to the means/ends logic that capital thrives on. Workshops like composting and you, wind turbine workshop, and soil: the interface of life provided opportunities to emphasize self-reliant methods to account for nature, food, and ultimately, each other. Juxtaposed with the pink cans of Campbell's soup, the spirit of generosity and ecologically driven sharing in Soil Kitchen was on a much smaller scale. But it was also more intimate and operated on a different set of principles. The win-win was not calculated in terms of sales, but instead in terms of enthusiasm, support, sharing, and giving.

BOOM YEARS FOR GIVING

It's the twenty-first century and giving—whether as a massive advertising campaign, an NGO providing health care in Africa, or an artist highlighting forms of exchange as art—is very much on people's mind. The phenomena of benevolence has manifest of late in an increasing constellation of forms. Giving to disaster relief. Giving to a homeless person. Giving at a charity ball. Giving to a neighbor. Giving to stop climate change. Giving as an artwork of social experience. A primal part of our social being, the human action of charity is not only a private encounter, but also a public project and a big business. It can be intimate. It can be collective. It can be earnest. It can be manipulative. In general, giving tends to be a little bit of all of this.

The early ethnographer of giving, Marcel Mauss, in his seminal book, *The Gift: Forms and Functions of Exchange in Archaic Societies*, makes quite clear the complex fundamental role that exchange and gift giving provided in what he referred to as "archaic societies," and within that, provided a contribution to the interpretation of exchange in contemporary society. Mauss understood that as in all economies are exchange based, the giving and receiving of gifts in the societies he studied were bound up in a complex arrangement of power, reciprocity, obligation, and an overall sense of the needs of the group. While contemporary capitalist life has more or less made all forms of exchange feel equal (equal meaning detached from the religious, cultural, and social obligations of the group and purely a mathematically decided relationship), Mauss disrupts this contemporary notion by pointing to different historic examples of exchange whereby gift giving reveals the complexity of the needs of the collective:

> We intend in this book to isolate one important set of phenomena: namely, prestations which are in theory voluntary, disinterested and spontaneous, but are in fact obligatory and interested. The form usually taken is that of the gift generously offered; but the accompanying behaviour is formal pretence and social deception, while the transaction itself is based on obligation and economic self-interest.[97]

To the question of charity, Mauss introduced the Chinook term *potlatch*. Rather than just a gift out of benevolence, potlatch was the custom of overwhelming an adversary or rival with an abundance of riches. Potlatch is a gift so large that it can never be returned and thus demonstrates the unquestionable dominance of the gift giver. Rather than hoarding surplus wealth, potlatch and charity are forms of using that surplus to leverage power.

Charity remains an exchange. Even when nothing is wanted in return, the exchange is caught up in power, culture, and interpretation. If Marcel Mauss studied the complexities of archaic societies versions of exchange (and with that one could say, charity), the contemporary iteration becomes all the more complex in an array of global economies, advertising companies, and NGOs, to name just a few. While the acts of receiving and giving might be difficult to assess in terms of the operations of power, the image of giving and receiving may be all the more so.

Charity is a social need that expresses itself across a range of economic and personal encounters. In so doing, whether it is the helping hand of Mother Teresa alleviating suffering, the artistic use of charity to free up a space in the public where a sense of the civic comes to life, or perhaps, in the case of Campbell's soup, an advertisement of charity deployed for the straightforward purpose of increasing sales, an intimate human emotion and a deep social need propel our culturally driven consumer society.

The numbers bear this out. In 2013, total charitable giving was $335.17 billion in the United States, and steadily rising. A majority of that giving is private.

These numbers should not be surprising. From the very beginning of human civilization, the imbalance of power has weighed heavily on the human mind. Jesus made a big deal of it. Julius Caesar upon his death gave all his possessions, lands, and coins over to the Romans. And let's face it, Prometheus died on a rock for the philanthropic effort of giving fire to mortals.

And as much as giving has occupied people's minds, so too has the question of when exactly one is giving, and when one is simply pretending to give. Thomas Fuller, a chronicler of the lives of the wealthy in England in his book, *Worthies of England* (1662), discusses the highs and lows of charity. He writes that the wealthy, "having lived like wolves, turn lambs on their death beds, and part with their fleece to people in want."[98]

With so much money and energy currently dedicated to helping others on such a vast global level, we must consider the overall structures that comprise giving versus governing. For certainly, the question of giving must take into account the larger structural questions that might normalize a system of taking. Is a government, in essence, a form of giving or one of sharing?

But of course, the other end of the question is the vast amounts of giving and the preservation of systems that normalize taking. It may not be a surprise that levels of giving have exploded in the United States equal to the growth in the disparity of wealth, as unfettered capitalism provides not only incentives to give to nonprofits, but also for the uber-wealthy to demonstrate their largess through charity.

In July 2013, Peter Buffet, son of billionaire investor and philanthropist Warren Buffet, wrote an op-ed in *The New York Times* critiquing what he called, the "charity industrial complex." As someone who routinely dines and trades with the world's wealthiest, Buffet writes from a unique perspective on the realm of philanthropy. "As more lives and communities are destroyed by the system that creates vast amounts of wealth for the few, the more heroic it sounds to 'give back.' It's what I would call 'conscience laundering'—feeling better about accumulating more than any one person could possibly need to live on by sprinkling a little around as an act of charity."[99]

Conscious laundering. Buffet's claim that owners of wealth actually need their conscious cleaned has a nice ring to it. He implies that the playing field for financialization of the world produces the very problems that charities are trying to solve, hinting toward a critique of capitalism.

How much good one is doing with one hand while doing damage with the other is perhaps at the core of the questions regarding the efficacy of charity and the role it plays in larger forces of structural inequity. In the same op-ed, Peter Buffet taps into the larger colonialist desires wrapped up in those with privilege wanting to help those without:

> Early on in our philanthropic journey, my wife and I became aware of something I started to call Philanthropic Colonialism. I noticed that a donor had the urge to "save the day" in some fashion. People (including me) who had very little knowledge of a particular place would think that they could solve a local problem. Whether it involved farming methods, education practices, job training or business development, over and over I would hear people discuss transplanting what worked in one setting directly into another with little regard for culture, geography or societal norms.[100]

Colonialist-minded philanthropy has a long tradition. Think back, if you are old enough, to the wildly uninformed global hit song of 1984 by Bob Geldof and Midge Ure, *Do They Know It's Christmas*. It plays on the radio every Christmas season. Written with the intention to provide relief for famine in Ethiopia (most certainly soup was part of this), the song featured some of the biggest pop stars of the time (Duran Duran, Bono and Adam Clayton of U2, Sting, Boy George, Paul McCartney, Phil Collins, George Michael, Kool and the Gang, and many more) and became the number one selling UK single until 1997. It also featured some incredibly birdbrained if not outright colonialist lyrics (sometimes it's hard to tease apart being uninformed from colonialism). Having to do with war-torn and impoverished African nations, the song ends in the refrain "Do they know it's Christmas time at all?"

Such a profoundly naïve question says more about the singers than those sung about. Perhaps the better song would have a chorus that sang, "Do we know what we're singing about?" This who's who of 1980s rock sing out proud and loud their benevolence in an embarrassing crescendo. Do they know it's Christmas time at all? Even with burning sun and no water, what could be worse than not knowing it is Christmas? There you have it. One could argue that the rock stars knew that the song had colonialist-minded lyrics, but also knew that this kind of racist, cliché-driven music would raise lots of money to feed the black children of Africa. Perhaps when it comes to charity, all sins are permissible if the dollars show up.

But before I become too cynical, certainly, the industry of aid has done good. In disaster relief, such as the 2004 tsunami in Sumatra, the 2010 earthquake in Haiti, or the 2011 Japan tsunami, aid poured in from nations and individuals alike. While the distribution of this relief and its actual efficacy have been hotly debated, what certainly cannot be denied is the sheer scale of this support, which comes in a torrent of cash roaring into regions when massive geologic tragedies ensue.

Charity, of course, is not limited to moments of emergency either. The entire nonprofit and global equivalent, the NGO system, has gone through a massive boom as well. With a range of services provided from hunger to schools to museums, these institutions whose missions must be to give back to the community become a vast infrastructure of care, services, and cultivation. According to the Urban Institute, in the United States as of 2013 there were approximately 1.41 million registered nonprofits contributing nearly 905.9 billion to the economy.[101]

Much has been written on the ethics of these organizations and the aims of their aid. On the negative side, one could say that rather than simply alleviating suffering, organizations of charity also act as a critical part of an infrastructure that creates problems in need of relief. Much like the arguments regarding welfare, one could argue that charities produce vast dependency on charity, or one could argue the reverse, that the desperate need for private charity indicates a vast problem in the ruling system. One can also say that charity ultimately is meant more for the giver than the receiver, and that the ultimate aim of aid, to encourage self-reliance and autonomy, are not part of the charity industry.

But, of course, one can say that the aid industry is one of the few things out there supporting many people in need who are devastated by the effects of a widening economic gap and increasingly centralized resources. Rather than blaming charity for the ills of society, one can also see it as organizations and efforts to alleviate suffering, as many people do when they give.

It is not in the scope of this chapter to itemize the range of complex discussions involving the vast growth and interworking of charities. In fact, the industry is so broad that one might have trouble differentiating charity from basic social service. But with charity's ubiquity articulated, we can now turn to the vehicles of branding that have gravitated toward its clarion call.

CAUSE-RELATED MARKETING

Ultimately, in an age of vast marketing, the image of something and the actual thing itself become deeply inseparable—what Warhol intuited about the black, white, and red Campbell's can. Now charity and the image of charity are, like it or not, inextricably tied. Thus, as opposed to trying to find the actual act of charity removed from the image of charity, one has to, instead, consider the dynamics of charity in an age of vast intimate spectacle. Such a spectacle happens not only in the world of incredibly large structures ranging from McDonald's to Amnesty International, but also in the small-scale moments of giving between friends and strangers.

Attaching causes to marketing is not new of course. Edward Bernays himself used charity to bolster a brand's position. Highlighting a product's social benefits was part and parcel of his campaigns for cigarettes, which promoted feminism and weight loss. Connecting health benefits and social causes to an advertising campaign is perhaps just one step removed from connecting charity to an advertising campaign. It is a win-win, as they say.

In the twenty-first century, this win-win has a name: cause-related marketing (CRM). In their book, *Brand Spirit: How Cause Related Marketing Builds Brands*, Hamish Pringle and Marjorie Thompson define CRM as, "a strategic positioning and marketing tool which links a company or brand to a relevant social cause or issue, for mutual benefit."[102] The pink-hued Campbell's soup can is just one example of a vastly growing body of marketing techniques that have figured out that charity work is also media work and vice versa. If a corporation gives to charity, the thinking goes, they should get their deserved media mileage. It doesn't take a media expert to notice to the growing body of cause-related corporate advertisements. The month of pink is just one very specific example. One would be hard pressed to find a corporation that doesn't advertise the good it is doing, from Walmart's Miracle Balloon campaign for the Children's Miracle Network Hospitals to GAP's RED campaign that raises awareness and donates 50 percent of profits of its RED products to HIV/AIDS causes in Africa (while simultaneously being considered a major user of sweatshop labor).

One of the longest-running cause-related campaigns belongs to the golden arches. The Ronald McDonald House began in 1974 as a unique partnership between a Philadelphia Eagles' player Fred Hill whose daughter had leukemia, the Eagles' general manager Jimmy Murray, the regional manager of McDonald's Ed Rensi, and Dr. Audrey Evans, the head of the pediatric oncology unit at Children's Hospital of Philadelphia. The Eagles were raising money to help their player Fred's daughter and approached the children's hospital where she was being treated with a donation. Dr. Audrey Evans had already conceived of a nonprofit idea whereby families of children with serious illness could have a "home away from home" while their children received care. The idea captured the imagination of the Eagle's owner Jimmy Murray and in his wisdom, he approached the local McDonald's chain to see if the proceeds from Shamrock Shakes could support this initiative as well.

By 1986, the hundredth Ronald McDonald House was built in the United States, and by 2010, the number totaled 300 with chapters in more than sixty countries. The Ronald McDonald House also established the Ronald McDonald House Charities (RMHC) charity (a charity, if you will, housed inside a charity), providing scholarships as well as a mobile-lab care unit. Quite quickly, RMHC became an entity unto itself whose connection with the not-so-healthy offerings of Mickey D's was clearly not without its ironies. That said, without a vast structural analysis of economics and quality of life, it would be hard to argue against the singular Samaritan work of the Ronald McDonald House itself.

But of course this act of charity by those who sling GMO-laden fast food at low prices with barely livable employee wages can't help but stick in one's throat. The paradoxes of cause-related marketing can be overwhelming.

The first use of the term "cause-related marketing" appeared in 1983 when American Express offered to provide one cent to the restoration of the Statue of Liberty each time someone used the card.[103] Patriotic, monumental, and in the spirit of giving, this initial CRM campaign demonstrated that giving could bolster the image of a company while helping the world at the same time. That campaign paved the way for future CRMs as it generated $1.7 million in funds for the Statue of Liberty, a 27 percent increase in card usage, and a 10 percent increase in card applications.[104] In the corporate advertising world, this campaign was a success by all measures.

Suddenly, the corporation projects more than just sales or image as its central reason for existence. It provides a deeper purpose. While corporations have been singled out legally as persons under the Fourteenth Amendment, the implication of their personhood was also decided in the court of vast cultural representation. For a brand to be a person it must also possess a soul. And as Pringle and Thompson indicate, in the fight to cut through the clutter of a vastly overwhelmed public, the appeal to do good is a strong one. That is to say, a product must have more than just a positive image. It must have a good heart. One must trust the soul of a brand, not just what it reminds us of, or actually does. Thus a vast array of social causes—from breast cancer to clean energy, from fixing the Statue of Liberty to flying doctors across borders—enter our consciousness through the steady stream of marketing we consume every day.

Through the 2000s to today, CRMs have become a staple of the marketing playbook. Just a cursory list of CRMs can tell a unique story of the world of charity that we currently reside in:

1997   Visa's Read Me a Story campaign

2004   Dove's Campaign for Real Beauty, a campaign to inform 5 million young women by 2010 about positive body image

2004   Whirlpool and Habitat for Humanity provide whirlpool products, such as a refrigerator and stove, to future Habitat for Humanity homes.

2007   Singapore Airlines partners with Doctors Without Borders to auction seats for doctors to travel.

2010   Pepsi Refresh, a campaign that donated $20 million to community-based projects doing good in an open platform open call.

2011   Hockey for Huggies, National Hockey League donates diapers to mothers in need

2013   #Hanesforgood: Hanes clothing company pro-

vides socks to homeless: a partnership between
Salvation Army, Hanes, and Mark Horvath of
Invisible People

Typically, the strategy has been to partner a corporation or brand with the do-gooder efforts of a nonprofit.
You don't have to run a nonprofit to understand how such
organizations could be desperate for influxes of money to
continue their missions. So the boom years for CRMs have
also been boom years for the nonprofits they partner with.
Doctors Without Borders, Amnesty International, and
countless others have departments dedicated to appealing
to corporations to establish mutually beneficial partnerships through CRM.

AT FAUST'S TABLE

So are CRMs a pact with the devil? Can a fruitful relationship spawn from the collaboration of a corporation and a
nonprofit or NGO? If you asked Doctors Without Borders if it is unethical for them to partner with Singapore
Airlines to provide seats to their doctors, their development officer would roll her eyes. In the landscape of global
capital, one is tempted by increasingly Faustian bargains,
and for many of those trying to combat inequities in the
world, it is a question of weighing the costs and benefits.
For Doctors Without Borders, when dealing with issues as

urgent as disease outbreaks and infant mortality, the small compromise of working with a corporate partner such as Singapore Airlines would be a no brainer and the criticisms would seem academically Marxist. But of course this is a matter of degree.

One could make a scale with the axis placing on one side the embarrassing paradox and the other, complementary partnerships. An airline company providing seats to doctors may not have the same ethical sting to it as say, a sweatshop-using clothing company having a charitable campaign to treat AIDS in Africa, or even more flagrantly, an ecological campaign by an oil company. In terms of the content of charity, some CRMs possess more flagrant contradictions than others.

As Peter Buffet noted, charities/philanthropy are often put forth by those who are fully vested in the system that creates the problems one is trying to solve. To spell the contemporary conundrum out more clearly: if capitalism is, in fact, that system that is producing many of the ills that charities are trying to ameliorate, then aren't CRMs a conflict of interest? How does one square the knot between partnering with corporations and doing humanitarian work? And in such a complex world, where partnerships between NGOs and corporations and the wealthy can obscure the overall effects of corporations and NGOs, are these partnerships more of a result of an industry of charity trying to grow while no one is able to take responsibility for the big picture?

It is not an easy question to answer, but it is the question that haunts most forms of charity/exchange/philanthropy. Giving, it seems, not only has a visual element, an intimate element, but also participates in a large ecosystem of capital. In his book, *Capitalist Realism: Is There No Alternative*, Mark Fisher posits that under neoliberalism, there is no way to produce alternative social structures. That the answer to capitalism, under the current conditions of capitalism, are often found in utilizing more methods of capitalism. What is the answer to the energy crisis for example? In the United States, the answer has been the mega-industry of fracking. This question is at the very heart of CRM. Can one use capitalism to overtake capitalism?

The 1998 Reebok Human Rights Now! tour in partnership with Amnesty International offers a compelling example. A marketing campaign designed to attract a young sports-gear-wearing audience, this sixteen-country tour took place on the anniversary of the fortieth anniversary of the United Nations Declaration of Human Rights. Reebok spent $10 million on the tour, equaling 90 percent of the marketing, and hosted a press conference in each city. The tour featured an impressive roster of what might described as "ethical" rock stars, such as Sting, Bruce Springsteen, Tracy Chapman, and Peter Gabriel.[105] After the tour, the commitment to the cause continued: the company partnered with Peter Gabriel and Lawyers Committee for Human Rights to initiate a program called Witness that gave video cameras to activists around the world. Witness has since become an international success story in the activist community providing open platform media to many of the most undocumented injustices across the globe. To be simple, as cynical as one might want to be about the marketing origins of this campaign, it nevertheless produced incredible social-justice results. To effectively untangle the knot that is cause-related marketing, one has to appreciate this kind of complexity.

GIVING AS FORM: GENEROSITY IN THE AGE OF POTLATCH

The desire to do good has certainly found its way into contemporary art as well. While that history is long, over the last twenty years the sheer scale of these efforts is of unique consequence. A veritable landslide of artistic projects has emerged whose entire modus operandi could be categorized, if not defined by, charity (we will complicate the term soon enough). Just as the uses of the social in contemporary art—ranging from relational to participatory—have arisen in tandem with the rise of the move toward the social in marketing, so too has the interest in charity in art (with charity actively being a catch-all term) emerged in concert with the growing uses of cause-related marketing.

These correlations are not accidental. Economic shifts and increased media saturation have altered the emotional needs of the vast consumer audience, which have then expressed themselves through art. As Ted Purvis writes in his book, *What We Want Is Free: Generosity and Exchange in Recent*

Art, "As the world's economic and social systems move ever more deeply into a relations of capital, it is very natural to look at social systems that emphasize other priorities."[106]

In 1992, as part of a seminal exhibition by curator Mary Jane Jacob titled *Culture in Action*, the art collective Haha created a storefront hydroponic garden that grew vegetables for people with HIV and AIDS. Kale, mustard greens, collards, and Swiss chard were made available in biweekly meals. The storefront played host to a series of public events including talks, workshops, activist meetings, and alternative therapies. It became not only a catalyst for doing social good, but also a place in which to build community. The storefront remained open for three years.

Certainly, this artwork by Haha resonates with the Soil Kitchen by Futurefarmers enacted nineteen years later. Over that period of time, so many more projects have come to life. I have not only chronicled many of them, but also participated in many projects' production. At times referred to as socially engaged art, these works often balance social justice with artistic practices that use the social to produce new forms of community and collective imagination.

Most artists involved in socially engaged art would bristle at the notion of charity. With a long history of pedantic colonialism attached to it, charity lays bare the imbalances of power operating in any exchange, and results in a sort of potlatch which keeps the donor in a position of power. As opposed to being a method of heightening the capacity of those being "helped," the relationship is often considered one-sided.

Our culture greatly desires the image of helping. This is to say, as much as one might bristle at the notion of charity, the complexities of these relationships remain intact, and in fact, it is productive to put them into conversation with a larger sphere of mediated culture where the image of charity is an increasingly useful device for consumerism.

ONLY THE TRUMPET'S SOUND REMAINS

It's impossible to avoid biblical references when discussing charity, perhaps because the Catholic Church itself is one of the progenitors of philanthropy. But the fundamental biblical texts are chalk full of discussions not only on the role of charity per se, but also on the way one should behave when enacting charity. Mathew 6:1–4 states, "Beware of practicing your righteousness before other people in order to be seen by them, for then you will have no reward from your Father who is in heaven. Thus, when you give to the needy, sound no trumpet before you, as the hypocrites do in the synagogues and in the streets, that they may be praised by others. Truly, I say to you, they have received their reward. But when you give to the needy, do not let your left hand know what your right hand is doing, so that your giving may be in secret. And your Father who sees in secret will reward you."

Twenty-first-century philanthropists have embraced the sound of the trumpet that Jesus suggested they mute. The sound that states to the world that one has been a very magnanimous person, a kind person, a person worthy of attention and goodwill is the benefit one gains from being perceived as charitable. It is an image. It is a perception. It is the pink color splashed over the breast-cancer-awareness Campbell's soup can. It is the verdant green that accompanies British Petroleum. It is the red in Gap's Red campaign.

In a world of cause-related marketing, it is not sufficient to dismiss the desire to do good as merely a marketing ploy. Nor is it sufficient to accept on its face the image of that doing good. Instead, what we find is again a conflation of scales and effect. For, being the intimate creatures that we are, we have an instinctual desire to understand the world through our personal relationship to it. When we see a pink soup can for breast cancer, we immediately understand that breast cancer is a bad thing, and this can is in some way doing something about it. Rather than place this soup can in the context of the actual finances of Campbell's, or consider its relationship to the global economy, wages, and health, we react on an affective level. We *feel* its importance. CRMs strategically tap into our most essential, feelings-based worldview.

We depend on stories to order our world, but when it comes to the complex capitalist system, the story is lackluster. It's not even a story that can be told. There are far too many protagonists, ethical gray areas, and in the age of marketing, even the image of all things from doing good to being social must be contextualized. Thus, the difficulties of reducing the image of charity to one of right and wrong. Instead, we certainly can appreciate the overarching atmosphere of coercion that surrounds these efforts. As brands search for souls and souls search for brands (people start branding themselves), the role that charity plays will only increase and its relationship to the image versus action will become more troubling.

As brands and people continually work toward ways to mean something to each other, we reach a horizon of co-ercion and communication. In the ascent of culture, that which produces meaning will inevitably become a fecund terrain which marketing will harvest. It often leaves be-hind a jaded realm of people feeling confused and distrust-ful. If helping people is actually hurting people, then what is one to do?

Artists have certainly taken notice of the contemporary contradictions in charity, and have found that in small mo-ments of genuine exchange, we find affective power. We find this rare experience of connecting, helping, being to-gether. Perhaps, in a perverse way, the more the powerful uses cultures for the purposes of coercion, the more people will find interest in art that focuses on the most basic emo-tional aspects of being human. Perhaps it would be bet-ter if this art is no longer interesting; it would be better if the scale and realm of social coercion were reduced sig-nificantly. Perhaps charity, rather than a battle of images or a fetish on the small scale, will no longer be necessary because governments simply take care of people. It's coun-terfactual but worth meditating on.

8

CORPORATE SOCIABILITY

IKEA, the Apple Store, Starbucks, and Other Corporate Annexes of the Civic

For children, play is life itself. For us, children are the most important people in the world, and the home is the most important playground. Play is a fundamental aspect of their development. Through this global research, we've gathered new insights about how play is perceived by children and parents all over the world.

These are the words of Maria Elander. She directs IKEA's children's school and is the mouthpiece for the corporate giant's education component. Yes, IKEA has a school. She is, no doubt, right. For children, she eloquently reminds us, play is life itself. It is the sort of truism that conjures feelings of both nostalgia and epiphany. Play is active. It is mobile. It is curious. It is participatory. And, at times, play is social. It ultimately takes a physical shape in the world.

When Elander references the importance of play, we can be sure her insight will intertwine with an elaborate mechanism of branding that moves from the realm of images into the kinetic and human space of the social.

I have so far mainly discussed culture as it exists in the form of media: a song on the radio, a mobilization of images or narratives that can be in the service of everything from entertainment to marketing. But ultimately, the power of culture resides in understanding that people are motivated by things they feel, fear, and enjoy; our affective relationships to the world greatly influence our decision-making. As Bernays, Ailes, and Nixon understood so well, people are social creatures. We, like children, like to play and interact with each other. So, working off of Maria Elander's perceptive description of play, this chapter will delve into the increasing value of the interactive spaces in the world of contemporary branding (and art). As an extension our eagerness to look at seductive images, we are also eager to immerse ourselves in fantastical environments that enact our desired human connections.

At the dawn of the twenty-first century, not only does the logic of cultural branding give shape to our cities, but it also manifests itself in the interior design of our most successful retail chains. This chapter will focus on three era-defining retail pioneers: IKEA, Starbucks, and the Apple Store. They owe much of their success to their common interest in producing social experiences—emotional connections that go beyond just shopping—in their physical retail spaces. As we will see, artists, as or-

acles, had already hinted toward our collective desire for
the social.

Walking into IKEA is an Alice in Wonderland–level
vertiginous feeling: down the rabbit hole and into a cata-
comb of rooms upon rooms. A veritable Disneyland for
middle-class living, the IKEA store blends fantasy, the social, and cheap cuisine in a wrap of stark yellow and blue.
The meals include, of course, meatballs and mashed pota-
toes with that fruity pink lingonberry sauce, but also there
are ribs, mac-n-cheese, carrot cake, and pudding. This food
is comforting. In fact, as warehouse-like as the IKEA experience is, it is strangely comfortable.

Even though IKEA is a corporate chain, their warehouse meets store meets living space appears to embody
the social-democrat ethos of its homeland, Sweden. When
Maria Elander evokes the desires of consumer society's
newest recruits, she also demonstrates a very Swedish
value. In Sweden, kids are of the utmost importance and
thus deserve to be taken care of and deserve play and deserve love. Sure, everyone says it, but Sweden's government
really goes for it. In Sweden (and let's all hope we are born
there), when a child is born, the parents are given fifteen
months of paid leave from work to divide up for the first
eight months of the child's life. Sweden has been at the
international forefront in supporting the United Nations
Convention on the Rights of the Child.[107] Parents of children under age twelve are entitled to 120 days of temporary parental allowance in the event that their child is ill,
or 60 days during the illness of the person who normally

takes care of the child.[108] These policies are actual civic commitment.

First, it is important to appreciate just how big IKEA is. IKEA is the largest consumer of wood in the world, singlehandedly responsible for consuming 1 percent of the world's wood supply.[109] As of March 2012, Forbes listed IKEA's founder Ingvar Kamprad as the fourth wealthiest person in the world (although it is difficult to ascertain the exact figure of wealth because the structure of the company is such that no one call tell just how much of it Mr. Kamprad owns). In 2012, 690 million people visited the IKEA store—that's double the population of the United States.

The appellation *IKEA* is, in fact, an acronym paying homage to both the founder and his bucolic Nordic origins. The *IK* is for the founder Ingvar Kampvrad. The *E* is for the family farm he was raised on, Elmtaryd, and finally, the *A* is for the name of the nearby village Agunnaryd. Despite being a behemoth of big-box retail, a strange, familial ethos permeates every aspect of its branding and design.

The chain came into existence in 1943, when young Ingvar was a mere seventeen. The store moved through a variety of permutations, beginning first as a catalogue business for home goods, opening its first showroom store for furniture in 1953, designing its own inexpensive furniture a few years later, and opening the first warehouse-style store in 1958. Ingvar had opened three IKEA stores before deciding to set up the flagship store in Stockholm at a mesmerizing 45,800 square meters in 1965.[110] By this time, the store had already gained a name for itself for inexpensive home goods and furniture.

In a perfect example of commerce mining the fertile land of culture, the design of the flagship store and its trademark maze-like layout was inspired by an early visit to the Guggenheim Museum in New York City. "We could do exactly the same thing: When we open in Stockholm, we could be just like the Guggenheim—we could construct it so we won't give them a choice where to go."[111] So wrote Ingvar. No personal choice, but a journey nonetheless. Ingvar is not a stupid man.

In 1958, IKEA introduced one of the core production innovations that stays with the company today: flat packing. Products are flat, and this maneuver allows them to be shipped at an extreme cost savings by filling up a shipping container to the brim. Ingvar believed that products should be as economical as possible, and that simple formula of keeping costs down would be the highway to financial success. But not only are the goods flat packed, they stay that way. The customer assembles the object equipped with an illustrated set of instructions that eschew the tedium of language itself.

As much as IKEA embodies all things Sweden, Kamprad fled Sweden in the 1970s in protest of its high taxes.[112] The company's general disdain for paying taxes is one of its more contemporary leanings, and IKEA has consistently maneuvered through tax havens and complicated internal structuring (a large portion of the company is ironically a nonprofit). According to a *Huffington Post* article, IKEA al-

legedly managed to cut its UK tax bill in half by sending
profits to another country in the form of payments to a sister company.[113]

LOW COST WITH MEANING

IKEA's vision statement reads, "Democratic Design: Low
Cost with Meaning." I will focus on the very last word in
this utopic claim: *meaning*. The construction of meaning
is, in fact, the sum total of the IKEA experience, a radical form of three-dimensional (perhaps even four dimen-
sional if one considers the time spent) advertising. It is
a space where meaning is produced—and by meaning, I
mean the construction of a person's taste, opinions, dispositions, and ultimately actions. Moving through the space
deeply impresses one emotionally, rationally, and through
lived experiences. And so, by meaning I mean culture.

IKEA's parking lot is massive, and the warehouse is an
overwhelming blue and yellow. By now, even getting to
IKEA is a sort of journey. Shuttles and even ferries bring
customers from far and wide, setting up amusement-park
expectations. When going to IKEA a person knows he will
spend a good part of the day there. She has already signed a
sort of temporal contract before entering the door.

Upon entering, one first encounters the eating area and
the children's play place called Småland, the place that Maria Elander spoke of so fondly. Småland is named after the

village in which Kamprad grew up. In each IKEA store, it provides sixty minutes of free childcare for parents as they shop. Småland typically comes equipped with a ball room, construction sets or puppet theaters, educational kids' videos, and child-care providers. According to the IKEA website, "Småland is a play area where children can feel Swedish forest atmosphere. While they are playing, you can enjoy your shopping experience knowing your children will be safe and cared for."

As one might guess, Småland is extremely popular. In a June 2009 article in *The New York Times* titled "A Cheap Date, with Child Care by IKEA," the writer emphasizes the connection between a sagging economy and this small bit of social assistance. "Over-stretched, money-conscious parents are using the store's supervised play area as their personal baby-sitting service."[114] The presence of childcare in a store in the United States is basically the equivalent of a luxury-service good. According to Jonathon Kohn, author of the 2007 book *Sick: The Untold Story of America's Health Care Crisis and the People Who Pay the Price*, "trusting your child with someone else is one of the hardest things a parent has to do—and in the U.S., it's harder still, because American day care is a mess. And about 40 percent of children under five spend at least part of their week in the care of somebody other than a parent."[115] But of course, this thing called childcare, a luxury service in the United States, is standard in many social-democratic states. In Sweden (the place that IKEA pretends to be from), childcare is a ubiquitous and beloved aspect of everyday life, found in stores, churches, schools, and libraries.

After dropping off the kids and having a nice cozy meal, parents embark on the circuitous journey of well-lit showrooms. Ingvar's research trip to Frank Lloyd Wright's Guggenheim inspired this winding road. While each showroom provides new possible designs for living, including bedrooms, living rooms, children's rooms, bathrooms, and kitchens, one nevertheless has no choice but to follow the singular, well-demarcated route. The experience is very much like walking through a commercial for better living. Customers lie on the beds, sit at the desks, and lounge on sofas, and whether they do so ironically, sincerely, skeptically, or enthusiastically, they all participate (because how can one not) in an adult version of playing house. Each experience is an opportunity to imagine these neatly presented home furnishings as part of their potential future lives. Sales people do not wander the floor. Instead, IKEA has service areas that you can approach if you have questions or need assistance. This way, the hypnotic spell of fantasy is never broken. It is a somnambulist drift, or perhaps a sensuous commercial made real.

The maze-like design of IKEA is purposefully meant both to guide the shopper's steps and to disorient his senses. One becomes lost in the twists and turns of the journey, and apparently such vertigo creates a mental state primed for what is known in the industry as "impulse buying." The visually tantalizing walking experience provides a lived-in sense of desire. Perusing buckets of affordable stuffed toys and children's rooms, one harkens back to early childhood memories. In grand kitchens one can dream of a family cooking and sharing a meal together. They are soft memories that make the shopper more amenable to that feeling that retailers are trying to manufacture: whimsy.

One can't help but think of the early shopping malls of the mid-nineteenth century, the Paris Arcades that so entranced the likes of Charles Baudelaire and Walter Benjamin. "These arcades, are glass-roofed, marble-paneled corridors extending through whole blocks of buildings, whose owners have joined together for such enterprises. Lining both sides of these corridors, which get their light from above, are the most elegant shops, so that the arcade is a city, a world in miniature."[116] As people strolled through the Paris arcades, much as they do through the IKEA store, they saw in each window the promise of future capitalism, as well as objects loaded with historical meaning. It made for a hypnotic, entrancing journey.

ACTIVATE

After the whirlwind journey of showrooms, customers are spit out into the marketplace. Descending stairs, they find a row of shopping carts and a familiar array of Swedish-designed household goods. Most customers come to IKEA to buy furniture (thus the showroom experience), but they first encounter aisles upon aisles of bowls, spoons, tumblers, vases, lighting fixtures, and faux plants—the very stuff of impulse buying.

It's like an elaborate entrance hall to enter into Walmart. Customers must first go through the hypnotic spatialized indoctrination ceremony to prime them up, and then they make their consumer fantasies come to life. It's not just shopping, but shopping done by a socially prepped and activated customer.

After the market, the customer is then again spit out into the warehouse. What was minutes before a fantasy world of lush showrooms is now a vast warehouse of flat-packed shelves with large bin numbers. The abrupt transition is like peeking behind the curtain. The customer is now in the raw industrial space where packaged goods have been off-loaded from sea containers on giant freighters from China. No longer just a customer, one is sort of a coworker. At this part of the ride, we, the customer, must participate in the construction of that world we initially walked through.

IKEA is a profound combination of utility and comfort. Somewhere between Carhart and pajamas. If the first image one sees is a kids' playground, the last thing one sees are cardboard boxes on vast steel shelving units. These shifts in somatic space come with equal shifts in the perception of the experiences themselves. And the last stage of that experience takes place far beyond the walls of IKEA.

As we all know, at IKEA's flat-packed furniture is yet-to-be assembled. The customer hauls the goods onto a flat shopping cart to finish the IKEA shopping experience at home. The customer, in finishing the work, not only provides savings for both producer and consumer, but also adds a value that perhaps not even Ingvar could have predicted. The customer, in essence, joins the IKEA team from the comfort of the home. A link of work is made between IKEA manufacturing to the assembly line of the living room. This form of cognitive association has been given the clinical name "The IKEA Effect" in a 2009 research study. "The Ikea theory suggests that when people use their own labor to construct a particular product, they value and love it more than if they didn't put any effort into building it."[117] The IKEA Effect. It has a nice ring to it. It is a kind of relationship building. You share in the creation, and you like the store more. It's a capitalist Stockholm Syndrome (country of origin connection purely a coincidence). The captured person feels sympathy for their captor. But such is the experience of us emotional beings. We can't help but establish relationships, connections, and emotional ties with those things we walk among, talk to, work with, and play with.

Brand development and advertising realize that not only do images leave an impression on us, but social and physical interaction do as well—perhaps more profoundly. This insight that people like places where they can play, laugh, be taken care of, and do work is obviously not lost on contemporary corporate culture and is a founding principle of the quasi-Swedish tax-evading corporation known as IKEA.

HANGING OUT AT APPLE

In the late 1990s, Steve Jobs was determined to change the public perception of Apple computers. He didn't like that third-party retailers like CompUSA and Best Buy treated Apple as just another product to be sold, as just a thing on a shelf with a price tag. Such interchangeability didn't sit well with the obsessive-compulsive man-of-the-year tech and marketing guru. He wanted Apple to be more than a product. He wanted his own Apple world. Despite the hesitations of his board, he pushed forward with plans to make what has now become the universally recognized Apple Store. Slick, glass exteriors, white lights behind the Mac symbol, minimalist design, hard Chinese-maple wood tables with dark blue–shirted helpers roaming around and people playing, talking, and mingling. These retail stores have dominated the shopping landscape over the last decade by pioneering the concept of a retail space that is more than a store. Today they stand as places of experience, of learning, of high design, and of comfort. They are sites of sociality.

In order to make his dream come to fruition, Jobs recruited a man by the name of Ron Johnson. Johnson, a Harvard-trained businessman, had risen to prominence through his fifteen years at Target retail design, where he changed the profile of the store from a K-Mart rival to a cheap-but-chic design showcase. He had turned the tired blue-light special into something more like *Project Runway* by inviting architect Michael Graves to redesign over 2,000

Target-brand household goods—shower stools, ironing boards, and toasters—using his signature sleek aesthetic.

When Ron Johnson came to Apple, Steve Jobs had created a secret warehouse to begin prototyping his future stores. He wanted a place where the selling of Apple could fit his own idea of what Apple meant. On May 15, 2001, the first three Apple Stores were opened, two in Tysons Corner, Virginia, and one in Glendale, California. The signature Apple Store look of linear hardwood tables and minimalist design took hold under Johnson's guidance not much later. He said:

> People come to the Apple Store for the experience—and they're willing to pay a premium for that. There are lots of components to that experience, but maybe the most important—and this is something that can translate to any retailer—is that the staff isn't focused on selling stuff, it's focused on building relationships and trying to make people's lives better. That may sound hokey, but it's true.[118]

Building relationships is a key feature of the Apple Store, and one that Ron Johnson knowingly included in his design. The key elements are knowledgeable staff, free repair services (the Genius Bar), and the reinvention of the point of sale, cash-register mode of paying. In order to foster these relationships, standard sales elements are deemphasized and reinvented to make the customer's interactions feel more natural.

For this reason Jobs and Johnson felt strongly that the staff needed to be knowledgeable about the Apple product and not only act as sales people, but people with a rarefied skill set to offer. Equipped with this knowledge in their heads, these people floating around the store possessed something that a customer would actually want. It was a way to begin a discussion. First produce the relationship, and then produce the sale. When a customer showed up with a myriad of questions about their computer (and like someone going to an automotive garage, the customer is anxious, in need, and generally out of their depth), the various blue-shirted first-name-basis salesperson stepped in. And this answering questions, produces, inevitably, a relationship. And not only a relationship, but also one where the customer had been vulnerable and then, magically, empowered.

Of course, this atmosphere of conviviality is orchestrated. Like an Orwellian dream, the attitudes, words, and dispositions of the Apple staff are well honed in order to appeal to the customer's too-human need for connection. Not that this is particularly new for any retail outlet, as employee-training manuals have always dictated the behaviors and public presence of employees. In the case of Apple, the tone was one highly calibrated for an attitude of empathy and assistance summarized in the handy acronym APPLE: Approach, Probe, Present, Listen, End. This set of instructions exists to assist the Apple Store rep in the art of listening and helping. The store's policies create an empathetic staff, whose employee handbook teaches them to relate to customers through the nifty alliteration: feel, felt, found.[119]

For example:

CUSTOMER: This Mac is just too expensive.

GENIUS: I can see how you'd *feel* this way. I *felt* the price was a little high, but I *found* it's a real value because of all the built-in software and capabilities.

If this style of management-speak strikes one as familiar, it is because everyday life provides a variety of similar examples, from hotel management to marriage counselors. The power of empathy leaves a mark and captures our hearts before our minds.

This emphasis on empathy and conviviality is only one part of an ecology of experience. The Genius Bar (a name that Steve Jobs couldn't stand) is the title for the free service-information center located in the Apple Stores. If the customer has more in-depth questions or needs something fixed on their computer, they turn to the Genius Bar. In addition to the Genius Bar, some of the retail outlets operate sleek classrooms where free workshops are taught on how to use particular Mac applications and devices. This all-encompassing offering of services in addition to products has earned the Apple Stores the description "full-service retail outlet," a model that has been replicated in tech stores across the board, such as the Geek Squad now operating at Best Buy stores (which aren't doing so well). It is all part of producing a cosmic space of assistance.

According to Johnson, "When we launched retail, I got this group together, people from a variety of walks of life. As an icebreaker, we said, 'Tell us about the best service experience you've ever had.'" Of the eighteen people, sixteen said it was in a hotel. This was unexpected. But of course: the concierge desk at a hotel isn't selling anything; it's there to help. "We said, 'Well, how do we create a store that has the friendliness of a Four Seasons Hotel?' The answer: 'Let's put a bar in our stores. But instead of dispensing alcohol, we dispense advice.'"[120]

There you have it, dispensing advice. A free service of interpersonal exchange with precedent in the labors of your everyday hotel concierge. More than anything Johnson's limited focus group reveals what people *remember* as their best-service experiences. A genuine interpersonal exchange in a sales environment produces a longer-lasting impression in the mind than an isolated shopping experience.

And how better to emphasize the social over the retail than to eliminate the cash register? If one wants to appear intelligent they may configure a living room so that it doesn't look like their entire lives are built around a television; Apple configured their store so it didn't look as though it was built around a cash register. Instead, the cash register became a personalized swipe from some mysterious iPhone-looking device arriving from the hip by a guy or gal whose name you not only knew, but who had already helped you. The cash register has become a person. That typical feeling of waiting in line to hand over one's money, and feeling acutely aware that the room is geared toward that very purpose, is gone.

Apple then shifted the point of sale toward one's own iTunes account or iPhone so that one could merely scan an item and purchase it on one's own. The retail outlet was there purely for assistance and knowledge, and the crass act of purchasing would remain in the hands of the consumer. Or so the design allows one to think. The interior-design decision to remove the focal point away from the cash register says everything about the Apple brand's decision to focus on relationships—while still pursuing the retail ethos of "Everyone in the Apple Store is in the business of selling."

For without a cash register, what is a room with people giving seemingly free advice? More akin to a library or high-school counselor than a retail chain, the Apple store became a site of social exchange. Add this to the fact that these stores were popping up in the real-estate boom years of vast urbanization, and we suddenly find a physical space that embodies the spirit of the age espoused by the likes of Richard Florida.

COFFEE: THE SINE QUA NON OF SOCIABILITY

Apple and IKEA are not the only retailers producing civic spatial experiences as part of their overall sales package. Starbucks has not only become famous for its skyrocketing sales and metropolitan omnipresence, but also for taking that simple thing called coffee and reaping the benefits of its ancillary social qualities. The Seattle-based corporate coffee chain has become known for emphasizing experience as its dominant and most important product. Their stated mission is "to inspire and nurture the human spirit— one person, one cup and one neighborhood at a time," and goes on to emphasize its relationship with its customers, "when we are fully engaged, we connect with, laugh with, and uplift the lives of our customers—even if just for a few moments. Sure, it starts with the promise of a perfectly made beverage, but our work goes far beyond that. It's really about human connection."

Starbucks got its start from the Berkeley of the 1960s. The three founders, Jerry Baldwin, Zev Seigl, and Gordon Bowker met while at school at the University of San Francisco. There they learned the fine art of roasting coffee beans from a Dutch transplant, the man who is credited with bringing artisanal coffee to the United States, Alfred Peet. Peet opened Peet's Coffee in Berkeley in 1966, and the Starbucks' founders opened their store in Seattle in 1971.

Just as David Geffen is getting ready to take over music, these pioneers of home-roast beans were gearing up for some global dominance (well, their journey would take longer). While over the next decade coffee sales in the United States declined, Starbucks and their roasted beans churned a small gradual profit. In 1983, the Starbucks' founders sent their ambitious head of marketing Howard Schultz on a business trip to Milan, where Schultz witnessed the café culture of espresso bars that are the quintessence of Italian life. Where the Italians had a community, Schultz saw opportunity.

Upon his return, Schultz implored Starbucks to open an espresso bar, but the board refused. In response, Schultz left the company to start his own Italian knockoff called Il Giornale. You might never have heard of Il Giornale, but that's only because it became so wildly successful that Schultz soon bought the Starbucks brand away from its hippie progenitors. In a peculiar twist of fate, the original team focused on Peet's Coffee, the company they purchased from their mentor in 1984.

Besides the *Moby-Dick*–inspired name and the artisanal roasted coffees, the Starbucks of today is the creation of Howard Schultz. The rise of Starbucks from the din of left coast Pike Place in Seattle to the signature icon of corporate-gone-green globalism is both a story of entrepreneurial acumen and good timing. Schultz brought about three critical shifts in the Starbucks model that provided the platform for unprecedented growth (Starbucks went from a $2.6 billion company in 2001 to a $16.4-billion-dollar company in 2014).[121]

The first transformation he culled from the café's of Milan. He wanted the espresso bar with its steam; its glistening mechanics; its rich, dense coffee aroma; and its made-to-order interpersonalism. He wanted that sense of community to pervade his café because he realized that the place to go to was more important than the drink—which countless Americans made for themselves quite cheaply each day. He felt the espresso bar provided that inroad.

The store is meant to be an experience, and Starbucks' handbooks, much like Apple's, reflect an attitude of performed empathy. The Starbucks' version of this ethos is called the Five Ways of Being: 1) Be Welcoming, 2) Be Genuine, 3) Be Considerate, 4) Be Knowledgeable, and 5) Be Involved. These five designed attitudes encourage the workers to be friends with the customers, to be involved in their communities, to give feedback on the running of the store, and to be as knowledgeable as possible about coffee.

Schultz also wanted the growing Starbucks stores to be everywhere and to provide a consistent brand. As Starbucks spread to different cities, Schultz refrained from franchising and instead opted to place stores in close proximity to each other under one corporate management. Since they belonged to the same company and were controlled by the central office, they were not in competition. Instead, ubiquity was the modus operandi. This strategy of clustering allowed the coffee shops to take hold of hip sections of major cities and then multiply. As we discussed earlier, urban gentrification's connection to Starbucks is a strategy, not an accident. The strategy existed not only for the purpose of beating out local coffee shops, but also, and perhaps more important, to spatially advertise themselves. Because the coffee shops were suddenly in hip areas, this presence, which had to be noted by anyone walking by, filled in for the strangely low amount of advertising. Schultz felt that word of mouth and sheer real-estate presence could substitute for the vast quantities of advertising dollars that most chain stores relied on. That is to say, why buy a billboard when you could replace one with the real thing?

Of course, Starbucks didn't invent the social aspects of coffee; that tradition dates back to fifteenth-century Turkey. Ethiopian Sufis discovered this delicious caffeinated drink, then, in the sixteenth and seventeenth centuries, it spread throughout the Arab world and into Italy and Greece. A seventeenth-century French traveler Jean Chardin provided an early account of a Persian coffee shop: "People engage in conversation, for it is there that news is communicated and where those interested in politics criticize the government in all freedom and without being fearful, since the government does not heed what people say. Innocent games . . . resembling checkers, hopscotch, and chess, are played. In addition, mollas, dervishes, and poets take turns telling stories in verse or prose."[122]

Popularized throughout Europe, coffee and its spatial extension, the café, have continued to embody the spirit of civic sociality through centuries of caffeine-high conversation. The first coffee shop in France opened in 1672 by Pasqua Rosée, who brought the fine drink over from London. Opening on the heels of his coffee shop came Café Procope, whose reputation and clientele is legendary, and often credited as a catalyst for the Enlightenment by fueling the chatter and banter of Rousseau, Voltaire, and Diderot. In eighteenth-century London, Benjamin Franklin frequented London Coffee House, where he discussed ideas with his Club of Honest Whigs. Café culture has long been synonymous with Paris, and images of Jean-

Paul Sartre and Simone de Beauvoir come to mind, sitting in postwar France at Les Deux Magots in the quartier of Saint Germaine des Prés arguing over women's rights, the liberation of Algeria, and the destitution of the singular soul. Ernest Hemingway working on a novel about anarchist revolutions against Franco. Picasso, James Joyce, and Bertolt Brecht enjoying a sip of espresso while in heated discussion. So many great books, art, and philosophies emerged, in part, out of caffeine-fueled synaptic eureka moments and epochs of urban excitement. More important to this narrative, cafés are part of our collective mythology about urbanism and our romance of bohemia.

That promise of bohemia ingrained in our notion of the café, in essence, became Starbucks' brand. Coffee isn't just a drink, it is a place where people and ideas come together. And while Starbucks' mission embraced experience as its primary value, its brand of bohemia benefitted greatly from a renewed interest in the urban as well.

When Starbucks says their mission involves human connection, they are being straightforward. It is no accident that the signature brand for what is called "The Experience Economy" is built on a beverage whose historic role went in tandem with urbanism and sociality. It wasn't only that Starbucks built up coffee as something to drink, but also, and more important, that the rise in Starbucks paralleled the rise of the privatization of social experience. Coffee and hanging out in the city have been a part of the glue of urbanism for hundreds of years—what Howard Schultz witnessed in the streets of Milan. Starbucks isn't selling a product, but a set of social relations—a way of inhabiting your city and your world.

ART GOES SOCIAL

Before multibillion-dollar corporations fully realized how to re-create and monetize the social, contemporary art understood the affective power of social exchanges. Focusing in particular on experience as an artistic medium, artists found themselves drawn toward situations that highlighted communication, intimacy, and sharing. By the twenty-first century, the bombardment from advertising and its younger cousin, branding, had become impossible to escape, and thus experiences free of this influence became more desirable. How is an artist supposed to communicate when the world is trying so hard to steal everyone's attention?

The story of a social-interpersonal art is quite long (too long to state here, even only the social-interpersonal contemporary art). Nevertheless, as a conclusion to this chapter on the retail world's fascination with and production of social space and relationships, contemporary social art allows us to see how the growth of cultural production created a desperate need for interconnectedness, and how, as a result of that desperation, new forms, and economies, emerged.

Referred to as "the dematerialization of the art object"

in the 1960s, this interest then sprouted into various genres, like Relational Aesthetics in the 1990s and social practice and participatory art in the 2000s. The theorist and curator Nicholas Bourriaud, who coined the moniker *relational aesthetics* in 1999, placed the work squarely in reaction to the commercialization of the social in the information age: "Anything that cannot be marketed will inevitably vanish." Bourriaud's words echo those of artist Allan Kaprow's participatory—thus transitory—performances of the 1960s, called *Happenings*, embodying the spirit of participation and play. He writes prophetically in 1966, "The *Happenings* are the one art activity that can escape the inevitable death-by-publicity to which all other art is condemned, because, designed for a brief life, they can never be overexposed; they are dead, quite literally, every time they happen."[123] Over time Kaprow's *Happenings* would become more elaborate and would also be part of a larger interest in immaterial artworks in movements such as Fluxus.

This spirit of participatory artistic production would reach new heights in the 1990s. A cavalcade of artworks that focused on the social experience surfaced and gained much attention. Perhaps the ultimate example of participatory art is the 1990 artwork by Thai artist Rirkrit Tiravanija simply titled *pad thai*. The project is so simple that a nonart person might have trouble understanding what the art is. The project was to cook the traditional Thai noodle dish, pad thai, in the Paula Allen Gallery in New York City and hand it out to the gallery goers. Unlike a painting or even sculpture, this work was a social experience. The

Thai food ultimately operates as a vehicle to bring people together to share a moment. The art isn't specifically the cooking of the Thai food, but instead the social experience that cooking Thai food produces. It is this basic aesthetic shift that would sweep across the increasingly global contemporary art world.

Over the last thirty years, the arts have become increasingly familiar with this kind of work. The British artist Gillian Wearing came to prominence with her photographic series from 1993, where she stood on a busy corner in South London, approached strangers, and asked them to write on blank paper whatever was on their mind. The resulting photographs depicted a moment of collusion between the subject of the photograph and the photographer. It also opened up a space of empathetic connection through photography, a medium that has become increasingly coercive through its association with advertising.

In 2003, the Brazilian artist Rivane Neuenschwander produced the work, *I Wish Your Wish*. The work takes as its inspiration the cloth wristbands with handwritten wishes that pilgrims would attach at the gates of the Church of Nosso Senhor do Bonfim in Bahia, Brazil. The belief was that once these wristbands fell off from wear and tear, the wishes would come true. Neuenschwander's piece involved handing out wristbands with wishes from previous viewers of the artwork. Recipients then must write their own wishes down, and that bracelet will ultimately be worn by someone else. In participating in the artwork, one enters into an intimate social bond with other participants.

While some artists in the growing genre of relational, participatory, and social art were able to cash in through the gallery system, many others were not. The art world manages to eke out some dollars for anything that contains both scarcity and social capital. But, even for a commercial market ever interested in the new, collectors' desire to acquire unique objects of art that retain their value limits the growth of this field of experiential art.

The search for how to turn these social experiences into gallery sales would reflect the strategy of your modern IKEAs, Apples, and Starbucks. But for many artists, the critical component of their aesthetic practice remained its refusal of the logic of the market itself. These artists wanted gallery goers to find themselves, albeit briefly, in a space where the commercialization of that moment was not immediately evident. Unmonetizable moments that make us feel something have left public experiential art as one of the last spaces to feel untethered from culture as a tool of marketing.

THE MARKETPLACE AS THEATER

Certainly, there is more to IKEA than a kids' playground and delicious meatballs. There are the extremely cheap home goods with sharp design. At the Apple Store, well, there are Apple computers. And at Starbucks, there is that magical elixir of sociality called coffee. That is to say, the experience economy isn't purely about the production of experiences. It is an experience coupled with a product that occurs in space.

Yet in digging into IKEA, the Apple Store, and Starbucks, I have hoped to illustrate a set of twenty-first-century retail outlets who are not only booming financially, but also embody the shift to the production of social relations as critical elements of their financial model. Each offers a new sense of what I skeptically refer to as the "corporate civic." They are physical sites located in many major metropolitan areas whose financial model goes well beyond mere products. They are physical places where experiences happen, whether it is meatballs, working on one's laptop, or asking questions about Final Cut Pro. And what is at stake?

In developing the formal aspects of spaces that produce social relationships, these retail outlets push the selling of goods and services far past the limits of a simple commodity exchange. They dictate and commodify the terms on which we do what we do best: exist in the world as social creatures. These sites are major places where people encounter each other, and thus they are a large part of what constitutes the contemporary concept and reality of the civic.

And of course these three ubiquitous corporate giants are just a sampling of the array of corporatized social spaces that dominate urban and rural areas of the globe. Whole Foods comes to mind as another twenty-first-century retail chain whose organic, bistro aesthetic often incorporates a sense of the civic through community billboards and collective-dining areas. And the world of Disney (perhaps the looming pioneer of experience production) has not only exemplified this aesthetic in their theme parks, but also has branched out with a successful retail chain and unsuccessful city in Florida, Celebration. Barnes & Noble, after realizing Amazon was soon going to take over the book marketplace, decided to make their outlets more like comfortable cafes (often with a Starbucks) that happened to have books for sale.

The social turn in retail came with a myriad of business theories and economics books. In their influential 1998 book *The Experience Economy: Work Is Theater and Every Business a Stage*, the authors B. Joseph Pine II and James H. Gilmore provide insights into the rise of the three giants of the corporate civic. Their book sets the stage for companies to think of the work environment and retail experience as a theater. They encourage retailers to think of the layout of the store more as a theater set than as a showroom for goods. Don't think of employees as workers but as performers. "When a person buys a service, he purchases a set of intangible activities carried out on his behalf. But when he buys an experience, he pays to spend time enjoying a series of memorable events that a company stages—as in a theatrical play—to engage him in a personal way."[124]

Looking at the examples of IKEA, Starbucks, and Apple, we find highly successful models of this type of civic theater. Hiding the cash register, making the employee more of an advisee than salesperson, or asking someone for their name to write on a cup of coffee are all tricks for transforming a rote transaction into participatory theater.

Conceiving of the marketplace as a theater offers profound insights into the effective formal elements of turning a store into a peculiar social place, as well as the key role that the arts have had in shaping deeply coercive experiences. What we see at work in the corporate civic are refined techniques of affect, of emotion, of those parts of humanity beyond rational decision-making. Plato thought the arts should stay out of the social arena because they were, indeed, so affective as to undermine reason. Today, politics and capital have harnessed the power of the arts precisely for that same undermining ability. Affect can compel us to buy in to a cause, or to simply buy something.

9

THE EVER-SO-*PERSONAL* COMPUTER

If the evolution of cultural manipulation involves the increasingly affective appeal to our intimate desires, fears, and needs for social connection, then of course the computer would be part of that story. A device born out of on-and-off switches, it has taken time to mold itself into the sensuous appendage it now is. Yet, in the last forty years, this machine has come to redefine the entire spectrum of that which we call culture. So, let us take a step back and appreciate what the computer has become.

Once a device to operate alone, the computer has become the platform that integrates and mobilizes our sense of our entire social world. An interconnected web of friends, acquaintances, like-minded individuals, and even hostile adversaries, the social network epitomizes the power of the intimate in the context of public opinion. There, our private lives are very public, and simultaneously, our public worlds are seamlessly integrated into our private lives.

If by the mid-1980s, people were vaguely aware that computers were going to change everything, by 2016, the point is so evident it borders on the inane. Computers have altered the geopolitical and personal landscape so dramatically that each generation finds itself dizzy with an entirely new way of being in the world. A technological revolution that perhaps eclipses the power of the radio, and might contend with the invention of the printing press as mankind's most world-changing invention, the advent of the personal computer, and its concomitant social platforms, has made the intimate the dominant mode of public life.

As of this writing, there are roughly 2 billion smartphones in use on the planet (there are 7 billion people on the planet) and 3.5 billion people using the internet.[125] The number of Americans who regularly play video games is 155 million, and four out of five households contain a videogame system.[126] In 2013, a study revealed that one in four people on the planet use a social-network site, and that number is predicted to grow in the coming decade.[127]

And the story of computers is not only about sales, but also, and more important, about time and usage. A recent study revealed that "in the United States, people spend an average of 444 minutes every day looking at screens, or 7.4 hours. That breaks down to 147 minutes spent watching TV, 103 minutes in front of a computer, 151 minutes on a smartphones and 43 minutes with a tablet."[128] The age of the computer has ushered in the sudden radical transformation of our entire way of being.

FROM MISSILES TO MISSILE COMMAND

At what point did a computer stop being a series of flashing lights and circuit boards helping navigate nuclear missiles and NASA space launches and transform itself into something the average person spent their entire day with? And furthermore, when did it move from the gizmo in the home office to that soft extension of our bodies? This is the transition of interest here. The big boom of computers came when the technology jettisoned from the mother ship of government defense spending, and found its way into the mass consumer market. For much of the 1950s and '60s, computers remained a remote concept to the everyday consumer. They played an important part of the backdrop of science-fiction films where lights would blink and large junky robots would occasionally appear.

But it would take time to integrate the computer into daily living.

Silicon Valley, as it came to be known, would provide much of the groundwork. The 1956 move by Nobel Prize–winning physicist William Shockley, who had helped invent the transistor, from New Jersey to Mountain View, California, would have repercussions for decades to come. Shockley started Shockley Semiconductor Laboratory and aggressively recruited some of the sharpest young minds in the business. When the Soviet Union launched *Sputnik 1* in 1957, the event brought a wave of funding to the American space industry, including the one company that could make transistors.

Despite the company's success, Shockley Semiconductor would lose eight of his finest employees not long after. In a move that would come to define Silicon Valley (and certain economic patterns as well), eight employees, including Robert Noyce and Gordon Moore, who would go on to found Intel in 1968, left due to Shockley's paranoiac aggressive managerial style and the fact that he balked at the creation of the silicon-based transistor. The "traitorous eight," as Shockley later described them, would form Fairchild Camera and Instrument (later named Fairchild Semiconductor) and would capitalize on using silicon as a key material in the production of transistors. The company pioneered a production method called the planar process, which greatly reduced the cost of transistors. These technical innovations would pave the way for the revolutionary semiconductor that would allow a computer, once the size of refrigerator, to fit in the palm of your hand. And the reduced costs made possible a new breed of person: the computer hobbyist.

Silicon Valley would become the seat of empire in the information age. All the major companies would find their way to the area outside of Stanford University, which initially offered reduced land rates to get companies to move to the region. If a technology company wanted to succeed, they had to situate themselves south of San Francisco in the Santa Clara Valley. With this kind of critical mass, so came the inevitable paranoia around trade secrets, copyright infringement, and employees ditching one company to either start their own or work for another. Technical innovation could mean life or death for a company, and these cutthroat values would come to shape the personalities of its key figures into the twenty-first century.

Fairchild Semi-conductor would make history when they released the first microprocessor-based programmable cartridge home video-game system in November 1974. It came with eight-track-size plastic video-game cartridges that they called videocarts. While it sold 250,000 units as it hit the market in the first year, it would soon come to be eclipsed by the era-defining company of Atari.

Atari is the creation of a man enamored by arcades. He loved the little booths at sideshows, and that feeling of gaming meets they produced. The arcades were also, quite obviously, participatory. You could interact with them. A pinball game, for instance, could keep a person occupied for as long as their quarters would allow. Atari founder Nolan Bushnell's love for games and his proficiency at engineering led him to start the most important video-game system of all time.

Atari had already held a prominent place in the arcade market with its 1972 release of the game Pong. One white rectangular paddle on each side with a ball bouncing back and forth, this digital form of tennis was a huge hit in the emerging world of arcade games. Bushnell had ripped the idea off another less sophisticated, but groundbreaking, home video-game system, the Magnavox Odyssey. Atari's version caught fire, and its momentum increased during the 1975 Christmas season, when Atari released the home console of Pong, which connected to one's television.

This home console transformed perhaps the single most important technology of the latter half of the twentieth century, the television. Suddenly, the one-way relationship of image and sound had become interactive. The viewer had become a participant. For many Americans, the idea that one could actually do something to that static-laden monument in the living room was paradigmatically earth shattering.

Atari would come to define the late 1970s and early '80s. Video games and the Atari home consoles would be the first way mass consumers came to know the computer, but the technology's future was uncertain.

And while consoles like Atari would come to define the early 1980s, the Nintendo Entertainment System (NES) would take over in the latter half of the decade. Introduced in 1985 to the shores of the United States, after selling 2.5 million units in Japan, NES would come to dominate the video-game market. Their initial launch came with fifteen games, including Duck Hunt, Ice Climber, Kung Fu, and the ever-famous Super Mario Bros. In 1988, NES had sold 7 million units, and by 1990, 30 percent of American households owned one. And as we know, the Atari and NES were just the beginning for the home video-game system.

Parenting children has been redefined to include standing by as kids stare wide-eyed at a screen, game controller gripped tight, as they gun their way through hours and hours of the day. Bored commuters play some innocuous and highly repetitive game like Angry Birds or Candy Crush on their phones. More than just a thing for downtime, video games tap into something deep. It can be social if one played against a friend, but it can also be quite wonderfully solitary. Time can fly by as one moves from level to level; small achievements pumping dopamine to the brain in a never-ending virtual quest.

A COMPUTER FOR THE HOME

Video games opened the door to computer technology at home, but most potential users weren't yet sure of what one might do with a home computer other than perhaps use it as an elaborate word processor. Like video games, the story of the growth of the home computer and related software is also the story of a kind of market consolidation of the efforts of a hobbyist community. Bill Gates and Steve Jobs have become the face of the emergence of home-computing, and, like the tyrannical Graham Bell before them, they were obsessively competitive.

Bill Gates, much more so than Steve Jobs, was a coder. Born in Seattle, Washington, in 1955, his upbringing tracks the evolution of programming language. At thirteen years old, he was introduced to the bulky beige Teletype Model 33 ASR and gained access to some programming instruction at General Electric through a school program. Gates took to programming immediately and wrote his first program in BASIC that first year. By the time he started his own company Microsoft, in Albuquerque, New Mexico, in 1976, he was at the cutting edge of the field, and in the right place at the right time. But it was perhaps his other forte that made him a billionaire: his capacity to corner a market.

The amateur computer community is perhaps the unsung hero of today's deeply commercialized Microsoft/Apple landscapes. Connected not only by a love for exploring the possibilities of programming, but also through an ethics of open-source technology and sharing, the hobbyist community would evolve into the modern hacker community. Enthusiasm grew considerably after the release of the MITS Altair 8800 in 1975. An early version of a home computer, the chunky blue box with an eight-inch floppy-disk player was created explicitly to appeal to the home hobbyist. The headlines of the January 1975 issue of *Popular Electronics* reads: "Project Breakthrough! World's First Minicomputer Kit to Rival Commercial Models."

The MITS Altair 8800 gave Bill Gates and Paul Allen the platform to launch what would become Microsoft. Reading about the release of the computer, they contacted the makers, MITS, and said they had a BASIC interpreter (a code to make using the computer easier) for sale. MITS said they were interested. Using their homemade language

Gates and Allen got the Altair 8800 to print the word "READY" on a roll of receipt tape. Then they typed in "PRINT 2+2," and the Altair 8800 spit out the answer "4." Communication was a go. They had made the language that would turn a series of flipped switches into something intelligible, thus creating the communication program for the first home computer. It was an important historic moment. MITS bought the program on a one-year deal, and Gates and Allen wisely kept the copyright, setting a precedent for the idea of copyright and code that would shake the computer world at its core.

In a very telling rift, Bill Gates published in 1976 an open letter to hobbyists used to working on an open-source basis, demanding that they pay for the BASIC software. He writes, "As the majority of hobbyists must be aware, most of you steal your software. Hardware must be paid for, but software is something to share. Who cares if the people who worked on it get paid?"

While one can certainly relate to this lament, the complaints were leveled at a vast network of hobbyists who felt their own collective efforts had not only provided profound progress in programming, but also whose very ethics challenged Gates's capitalist approach. The key focus of Gates's attack was the Homebrew Computer Club: an ad-hoc gathering of electronics enthusiasts and engineers that would eventually not only establish the bedrock of Silicon Valley but would also spur the work of Apple Computers. At this point, the Homebrew Computer Club had in attendance the engineering and programming guru Steve

Wozniak and the now famous obsessive-compulsive Steve Jobs. Jobs had taken a position at Atari in 1974, becoming its fortieth employee. As legend would have it, he was such an obsessive pain with other employees that founder Nolan Bushnell set up a special arrangement for Jobs to work at night.

If Steve Wozniak was the more technically efficient of the two, Jobs was the Bernays. He was the marketer. He made technology personal. Jobs's 1976 decision to name their company Apple says more than anything. This was the era of consoles named the Altair 8800, or the only slightly more people-friendly Atari. Naming something Apple ran counter to everything that computers represented. And of course that was the point. The apple got us evicted from Eden. It was knowledge mixed with desire. It was a familiar fruit. It was homespun. Apple computers were not going to lead the field in terms of microprocessors and RAM speed, but they would in personality. While Bill Gates would literally make billions off of software for the home user, Jobs would emphasize that computers were extensions of people's desires, dreams, and bodies.

After releasing the Apple I (a computer designed famously in Jobs's garage), Wozniak and Jobs released the Apple II computer in 1976. While the first Apple was much more a kit of parts for the hobbyist, the second came to define the company and established a classic computer look. With the advent of a program that allowed one to do basic accounting, the Apple II crept into the home consumer market. While that market hadn't yet exploded into what we know today, "between September 1977 and September 1980 yearly sales grew from $775,000 to $118m, an average annual growth rate of 533 percent.[28]"

A giant leap for the computer industry came in 1984, one year after the crash of the video-game market and one year before Steve Jobs left the company he founded. The Los Angeles Raiders were playing the Washington Redskins in the Super Bowl when the 1984 commercial directed by Ridley Scott (fresh off his epoch masterpiece *Blade Runner*) hit the screens. The ad starts out with bald men in matching coveralls marching, drone-like, down a corridor. A blond woman in red shorts and running shoes comes rushing through the nave of rows and rows of these bald men who stare helplessly at a big screen on which a large man appears to be giving speeches. Most surely, this is the Orwellian big brother—it is, after all, 1984. Chased by riot police, the woman holds a giant hammer in her hands. She hurls the object through the air and it crashes explosively into the screen. In the blinding light, a text appears with a voice-over that reads, "On January 24, Apple Computer will introduce Macintosh. And you will see why 1984 won't be like *1984*."

While the Macintosh wouldn't fly off the shelves (it was far too expensive for the home-user market), it nevertheless embodied every aspect that would make Steve Jobs's reputation as the marketing and design guru. The commercial, for one thing, is a very powerful attempt to differentiate itself from not only IBM but also perhaps the lore of computers in general. It is Apple. IBM is the man. Apple is the extension of the human spirit and freedom. It's an early instance of a major marketing trope that positions corporations as the rebels. It presages Mac's "Think Different" campaigns, putting the computer in league with Jobs's hero Bob Dylan and difference makers like Mahatma Gandhi and Albert Einstein.

And while it is tempting to discount the advertisement as a ploy to strike that balance between consumer friendly and rebel, it is helpful to appreciate something more affectively powerful about Scott's commercial: in locating the spirit of the computer in the individual, the advertisement, and the personal computer itself, focused on the desires and needs of the intimate consumer. That is to say, not only did the ad present an image of personal revolution, but the personal computer would be the medium of that revolution.

The revolution would obviously not be an economic one, as Apple would toe the line, and eventually expand, the logic of capital. But it would be a revolution in behaviors, attitudes, and emotions. Bernays had intuited the deep connection between the private and the public, but it took nearly a century to make the technology that would synthesize that relationship. Ultimately the computer would revolutionize the individual's role in the matrix of cultural production.

The Macintosh was the first computer to popularize the graphic user interface and a mouse (Xerox had done it first but no one noticed). The computer came equipped with a word program and a paint program. Said another way, this was the first computer that emphasized touch and the capacity to make art.

Despite the original tenets of the Homebrew Computer Club, Jobs, like Gates, pushed to make these technologies, and everything about Apple, proprietary and limited. Jobs believed that consumers didn't really want options. They needed to have freedom, yes, but only inside a very circumscribed environment.

Ultimately, the computer ushered in a new era of culture as weapon. It is a weapon that cuts many ways. Our current moment resembles the advent of television in that we have seen an exponential expansion in the consumer market, but the computer is not only a device of reception, but also equally one of transmission. It is literally a tool. And Jobs emphasized that these tools could be extensions of the touching, feeling needy body. The touch screen as the extension of the hand. The iPod as the extension of the ear. The iPhone, the extension of our social lives. Apple didn't only bring the body into technology, but also brought these parts together entangling the body in a web of connectivity.

THE INTERNET

Understanding the complex world that the digital revolution has created requires an appreciation of the rise of the personal computer (and video-game system) and its parallels with the increasing reach of the internet. The origins of the internet can be found in some original memos written by J.C.R. Licklider in the early 1960s to the members and affiliates of the Intergalactic Computer Network, stating, "It will possibly turn out, I realize, that only on rare occasions do most or all of the computers in the overall system operate together in an integrated network. It seems to me to be interesting and important, nevertheless, to develop a capability for integrated network operation."[129] Not only was it prophetic, but it influenced generations of military scientists to come. Still the heyday of rock and roll and television, computers predominately existed in annexes of military and scientific research. It was a world of both science fiction and science grants.

Much of the early computer research took place at the Defense Advanced Research Projects Agency (DARPA), which was established by Eisenhower in 1958. A hive of the military brain trust, DARPA specialized, and continues to specialize, in the technological end of the U.S. military. Throughout the 1960s, the agency made gradual progress on an upgraded version of Morse code, whereby signals would be relayed electronically. If it seems shocking that the internet was created in the U.S. military, one must keep in mind that it is one of the few places where open-ended research could take place. There, Lawrence G. Roberts created one of the first iterations of the internet with the painful acronym, ARPANET. ARPANET already had the attention of a wide variety of military advisors including DARPA, RAND, and the British NPL.[130]

By 1972, the first electronic message would be sent, like a conference call between computers.

The first dial-up Bulletin Board Systems came into existence in 1978 (encouraged in large part by the affordability of the Apple II and S-100 bus machines computers which provided expansion slots) in Chicago. At this point, the technologies were the terrain of a handful of tech hobbyists. The early BBS logged 253,301 calls before it retired. These systems allowed early computer users to post information (like a bulletin board) that others would see. The growth of bulletin-board services, and the inherent problems that growth produced, would spur the increase in modem capacity.

As soon as it became possible to download a low-res image in GIF format from the bulletin boards, the early era of internet porn emerged—and every other sort of social activity. As MIT professor Sherry Turkle writes in her book, *Alone Together*, "So, for example, the ARPANET, the grandfather of the Internet, was developed so that scientists could collaborate on research papers, but it soon became a place to gossip, flirt, and talk about one's kids."[131] As affordability and availability of computers increased, so did the scope of these networks.

AN ANALOGUE DO-IT-YOURSELF

Different mass-produced technologies had already laid the groundwork for what the internet would eventually provide. Conviviality, sex, affinities, gossip, and bored banter are parts of the connective tissue that makes us who we are and structures our everyday lives. Let's start this conversation in 1991. It was a time before Friendster and before MySpace (let alone Facebook). It was a time before the popularity of dial-up modems and even e-mail. Everyone used landlines, and the closest thing to a cell phone was in war films or a rich person talking from their convertible into what looked like a transistor radio.

Beyond the digital revolutions of the bulletin board systems and ARPANET, it is also productive to see that the ground for social connection had already been laid by a growing community of cultural producers interested in taking the media into their own hands. Of course, the history of alternative media is very long. Paper Tiger Television in New York City emerged in 1981. One of its founders put its inspiration rather succinctly: "It is one thing to critique the mass media and rail against their abuses. It is quite another to create viable alternatives." Paper Tiger Television advocated an alternative to the mainstream capitalist-dominated airwaves. By sheer dint of its production costs, alternative television required much more gear and a reliance on the television airwaves. But it embodied a spirit of do-it-yourself media that would become all the more possible as the technologies of media distribution found their ways into the hands of the masses.

If culture throughout most of the twentieth century predominately moved in a direction from power to the masses, the twenty-first century has greatly expanded the capacity for multidirectional communication (the realities of this can be debated later). The distribution of photocopiers, eight-track recorders, audiocassettes, and radio-broadcasting technology made the ability for small-scale producers to be their media. Warhol's prediction for the future—that everyone would be famous for fifteen minutes—would come true once the technology became more cost effective. Rather than just watching rock stars, people wanted to be them. Rather than listen to radio, people wanted to be the radio. Rather than read magazines, people wanted to make their own. This is the era of do-it-yourself, and the capacity to take the production of anything from zines to mix tapes to radio programs was in the hands of the masses.

In the early summer of 1993, in the once-radical Berkeley, California, a bearded Stephen Dunifer crawled up into the Berkeley hills with the intent to break the control of the corporate radio media. It was the height of the first Gulf War, and Dunifer, fueled by his frustration with what he saw as a move to the center by major media including local NPR affiliate KPFA, had decided to take matters into his own hands. Thus began Free Radio Berkeley (FRB), a low-frequency unlicensed pirate radio station found at 104.1 on the FM dial. Dunifer sat on the top of the hills hoping to maximize his broadcast range and began what would become a movement across America to bring alternative news to the people. Radio, that device that had brought jazz and rock and roll to America, was finding its way into the hands of the everyday person.

Dunifer's revolutionary act was stoked by the increasing affordability of low-power radio technology. For $1,000 to $2,000, a low-power radio could be put into action. Free Radio Berkeley inspired hundreds of pirate radio stations across the country, with the FCC stepping in as their regulators, basically prohibiting independent shops from opening up. The battle of control over the airwaves was quite real, and by June 1998, after thousands of hours of broadcasting to the Bay Area, FRB had to stop broadcasting (at which point they turned their attention to the distribution of radio technology).

At the same time, throughout the 1990s, the zine culture gained tremendous traction. With the increased availability of photocopy machines, amateur muckrakers, journalists, cartoonists, and authors put their images and stories to paper and then, with a press of a button and the hot press of toner, they cranked out their tracts. Stores like Kinko's (which would eventually become FedEx Office) grew at an accelerated pace.

And with the growing affordability of four-track recorders, bands were more and more able to record albums onto tapes and distribute on their own. Hip-hop would have never reached its heights today if it weren't for the mixtapes that MCs recorded on audiocassettes and circulated widely by hand. Unlike vinyl records, audiocassettes were cheap. They could move from hand to hand and everyone had a cassette player.

Throughout the 1990s, a growing availability of technologies that could extend the voice of individuals was already reshaping communications. From pirate radio to mixtapes to photocopies, the modes of distribution were moving from a one-way relationship to one that moved more horizontally across networks. While certainly located in what would be called *subcultures*, these methods of communicating and expressing oneself presage the era of social networks to come. The true power of the new communication would be felt both in the United States and throughout the global left-wing community when a group of indigenous activists resisted the Mexican government at the dawn of 1994.

WELCOME TO THE JUNGLE

The Lacandon Jungle in the southern Mexican province of Chiapas and its indigenous community seem like an unlikely place and people to emerge as the poster child of a net-based form of social movement. The indigenous resistance that would become the Zapatista movement came out of a basic desire for the basic right to exist—they weren't interested in computers. By the time the Zapatista Army of National Liberation (EZLN) declared war on the Mexican government in 1994, they had already been hard at work trying to establish rights, land reform, and protection for the regional indigenous population since their founding in 1984. The movement was built on a strong sense of historical urgency:

We are a product of 500 years of struggle: first against slavery, then during the War of Independence against Spain led by insurgents, then to avoid being absorbed by North American imperialism, then to promulgate our constitution and expel the French empire from our soil, and later the dictatorship of Porfirio Diaz denied us the just application of the Reform laws and the people rebelled and leaders like Villa and Zapata emerged, poor men just like us.[132]

On January 1, 1994, uncoincidentally the day that the North Atlantic Free Trade Association went into effect, the EZLN declared war on the government of Mexico. Armed and clad in black ski masks, this revolutionary indigenous movement seized five towns. While historically, insurgencies like theirs would be routinely crushed by the Mexican government in a news vacuum, news of the revolution spread like wild fire. Tapping into an emerging network of NGOs, activist groups, and media outlets, all recently empowered by interconnectivity and internet-based communication, the Zapatistas called for the assistance from the international organizations sympathetic to their cause: "We also ask that international organizations and the International Red Cross watch over and regulate our battles, so that our efforts are carried out while still protecting our civilian population."[133] Not only were left-wing amateur reporters able to make their way into the jungle and side-step major media outlets in their reporting, but communiqués from the Zapatista top command circulated through a vast international network of sympathetic organizations through fax machines, e-mail, and phones.

The year 1994 was also the year the White House decided to get a domain name. It was the year the word *spamming* was invented. And it was one year before Compu-Serve, American Online (AOL), and Prodigy started to offer dial-up internet access. This was truly the dawn of social networking as we know it.

Twelve days of intense fighting broke out with then president Salinas throwing 12,000 troops with armored trucks at the insurgency coupled with airstrikes. And then, somewhat bewilderingly to analysts, they called a ceasefire. By all measures, they could have crushed the Zapatistas, but instead they decided to hold back. By all accounts, it was due in large part by a significant showing of soft power as public opinion. The Zapatistas, in other words, had successfully mobilized a social network to spread alternative informa-tion. The Zapatistas became the darling of a post-Soviet left and with it garnered the attention of the multitude of latent networks awaiting connectivity. But they also, through the mouthpiece of the charismatic spokesperson Subcomman-dant Marcos, eschewed a traditional communist platform advocating for autonomy and cultural specificity. Thus they were labeled the first postmodern revolution. Their rhetoric also allowed them to side-step easy labeling in the media and gain the curiosity of a vast global public.

It wasn't only left-wing activists and NGOs that took notice of the Zapatista revolution: so too did the U.S. mili-tary research organization RAND. In 1998, RAND published an in-depth analysis of the revolution, *The Zapatista Social Netwar*, penned by David Ronfeldt, John Arquilla, Graham Fuller, and Melissa Fuller. These researchers saw a particularly different kind of insurgency manifest in the Zapatista rebellion, punctuated by its use of, and dependence on, social networks. "A transnational network structure is taking shape, in which both issue-oriented and infrastructure-building NGOs are important for the development of social netwar."[134]

The researchers made the prescient analysis that social networks would gain increasing leverage in challenging the dominance of governments. They compellingly quote Foreign Minister Jose Angel Gurría, who states, "Chiapas . . . is a place where there has not been a shot fired in the last fifteen months . . . The shots lasted ten days, and ever since the war has been a war of ink, of written word, a war on the Internet."[135]

SOCIAL NETWORKING IN THE 1990S

The introduction to social networking for most Americans consisted of early chat rooms and dating sites. While businesses like CompuServe had provided platforms to communicate in relative real time in the late 1980s, it was American Online (AOL) that introduced a far broader audience to online communication. By 1993, AOL had surpassed CompuServe and Prodigy as the number one platform for home users to access the internet. This was the era where one paid by the hour for internet. By 1997, 18 percent of homes had internet and half of those used AOL.[136]

Much of the early movement around social networking came equipped with the online desire for dating and sex. The first dating site Kiss.com launched in 1994, followed by Match.com in 1995 (as of 2002, it has 26.6 million users). Identity-driven websites for dating also emerged, such as AsianAvenue in 1997 and BlackPlanet in 2000. It didn't take a psychoanalyst to see that when it came to the growth of popular use of the internet, sexual attraction would be its backbone.

So before we go straight into the rise and demise of Friendster, then MySpace, it is productive to take a brief detour down the road of porn. For the story of porn is central to the story of the internet. As Brian McCullough writes in his "A History of Internet Porn": "By August 1996, five of the ten most popular newsgroups on usenet were adult oriented; and one, alt.sex, reportedly served half a million users every day. In a *Time* magazine cover story on 'Cyberporn' in 1995, Phillip Elmert-Dewitt reported that 83.5 percent of the images on usenet were pornographic."[137]

Before we simply accept this information (today it is clear that internet porn is such a major part of the internet), one must appreciate its shocking history. Porn, perhaps in part due to its ability to actually generate an economy, but also in part due to its deeply intimate nature, is a critical part of the way our contemporary lives function. Porn amazingly precedes even the production of images on internet services. An early form of online pornography titled ASCII porn used text in an array, much like a pointillism painting, to create an image.

While porn has historically accompanied the rise in a given technology—from the printing press to the camera to early cinema—the scale of today's online porn economy is staggering. It is currently estimated that pornography accounts for nearly 30 percent of the money made on the internet. A 2011 study found that 70 percent of men aged eighteen to twenty-four visit a porn site at least once per month. And, the average age of first exposure to Internet porn is eleven.[138]

Pornography not only became the driver for e-commerce but it also shaped much of the technological innovations of online video. As the dominant internet commercial enterprises of the mid-1990s, porn sites also developed some of the earliest methods for tracking payments, having members log in, and also systems for locating fraudulence. And clearly, pornography strikes very closely to the manner in which the computer taps into the intimate subject. Not only is it a desire extender, but as statistics show, it is a desire augmenter.

THE WHOLE WORLD IS WATCHING

By the late 1990s, not only had the personal computer and the internet found its way into daily life, but the social implications of the internet were entering a publicly visible scale. The personal computer, with its distributive capacity and social connectivity, had begun to define the social texture of everything from dating to political protest. If the Zapatistas kicked off a sort of techno-anarcho sensibility among the international activist community, it would be further developed by an enthusiastic, and historically powerful, zeitgeist of artists, activists, and hackers.

Throughout the 1990s, the art collective Critical Art Ensemble produced books that espoused what they called "tactical media." It was a language of Yippie-inspired media sabotage that would infiltrate the systems of the powerful by using their very forms (for example, critiquing biotechnology by using biotechnology). While certainly rooted in the *au courant* tendencies of political art of the period, their books gained much traction in the emerging hacker and tech community.

Throughout the later part of the 1990s, an increasing number of conferences and online forums emerged with the intent of exploring and acting on the political possibilities of the internet. In 1995, during the international art exhibition, the Venice Biennale, a group of artists, activists, and media theorists under the moniker of Club Berlin gathered to discuss a critical approach to the possibilities of the internet. Out of that meeting emerged a long running e-mail LISTSERV titled "Net.time" (founded by Geert Lovink and Pit Schultz) that considered itself a counter to the American protocapitalist approach to technology. In 1996, the second iteration of the conference, calling itself

Next 5 Minutes, dedicated solely to tactical media, took place in Amsterdam and Rotterdam. Among the speakers were Critical Art Ensemble, Paper Tiger Television's DeeDee Halleck, Geert Lovink, and Pit Schultz. Many conferences would soon follow, and the interest in the social possibilities of the internet gained traction in tandem with a growing sense of international solidarity, as movements from across the globe gained easier access to each other.

In 1997, three years into the Zapatista uprising, the art/activist collective Electronic Disturbance Theater (formed by former Critical Art Ensemble member Ricardo Dominguez, Brett Stalbaum, Stefan Wray, and Carmin Carasic) was formed to produce internet-based civil disobedience. Their most renowned project took place in 1998 when they unleashed a web-hacking program called Flood.net, which organized the many online supporters of the Zapatistas to shut down the websites of anti-Zapatista forces, particularly the Mexican government. These actions gained significant media attention, and brought the use of civil disobedience on the web to the mainstream consciousness. Articulating their philosophy, the collective writes, "Artists as communications engineers, working in groups to design the next generation of networked communications pulse-weapon, will allow still larger groups to leverage their numbers in tactical performances of presence; these are the goals of non-violent infowar."[139]

To return to the protests against the World Trade Organization in Seattle in November 1999, the potential of the Internet had become clear. The mobilized web of NGOs, nonprofits, and activists that the RAND corporation anticipated came to fruition in what would be called the alt-globalization movement, and specifically in the launch of the Indymedia website.

What made the Seattle protest different was not only that it targeted a multinational trade organization (as opposed to a single government, for example), but also that it was accompanied by a web presence that allowed up-to-the-minute reports from the field. The Indymedia website utilized an open publishing script that allowed activists from around the world to witness a version of the news that certainly was not available in newspapers, radio, or television. As the police filled the streets with tear gas, protesters could be heard chanting, "The whole world is watching" and they didn't necessarily mean television. One cannot underestimate the power that this kind of shocking on-the-ground reporting had in terms of a shifting perception on not only this specific issue, but also on the power of alternative media.

The anti-WTO protests would be followed for the next few years by protests around the globe, loosely connected in an overarching push back on neoliberal capitalism. With that, Indymedia affiliates in cities blossomed. By 2002, there were eighty-nine individual Indymedia sites located in thirty-one countries. The social network anticipated by the Zapatistas had grown.

MYSPACE MELTDOWN

Of course, Indymedia and the Zapatistas aren't typically credited with the origins of social media. More generally the progenitors of social networking came out of the evolution of dating and friend sites. Websites such as Six degrees and Classmates, where a person developed a profile and invited friends to join one's network, offered the template of what would become a famous formula in the 2017 era of Facebook.

In 2002, the website Friendster launched with overnight success, amassing three million users in its first three months. Suddenly, people were finding each other online. A hybrid of locating long-lost friends, seeing what old classmates were up to, and of course, ogling the array of prospective romance, the rise of social networks unlocked a variety of social relationships that had previously been bound by the limitations of geography and communication. For founder Jonathan Abrams, the concept behind Friendster (a name derived from the combination of the popular music-sharing website Napster and well, the word *friend*) was to use one's friends network as a method to find a date. Abrams considered the project a competitor to Match.com, the preeminent dating site that was bringing in $73 million a year.[140] Friendster gained the attention of both users and investors. A *Fortune* magazine article in 2003 writes, "There may be a new kind of Internet emerging—one more about connecting people to people than people to websites." In 2003, Friendster declined Google's offer to purchase the site, believing that the network worked best in their own hands. After the dot-com bust of the late 1990s, social networking looked as if it might revive the internet economy.

In just a year, it would take nearly one minute for the site to load as the servers suffered from its success. Suddenly, Friendster founder Jonathan Abrams found his site freezing up.

In 2004, Friendster had gained a tremendous amount of investment money, Abrams had become a regular talk show guest, and the board had gained members from Amazon, eBay, and even CBS. And yet, the writing was on the wall. As Abrams toured talk shows, the site continued to be slow, and another social-networking juggernaut seemed to be drawing more and more people to its site. That site was MySpace.

In Homeric fashion, the epic rise and fall of MySpace offers insights into not only how the web works, but also how the demands of capital and advertising set the course for navigating the newly emerging cultural terrain that was the web 2.0. Poetically enough, the founders of MySpace (Chris De Wolfe and Tom Anderson) were working at an internet-marketing company, eUniverse, which predominately worked on producing pop-up ads for everything from skin-care products and printer cartridges and generating lists of e-mails for marketers—the back end of internet advertising. After the dot-com bust and in light of numerous laws against spamming, the two took inspiration from Friendster. According to ex–vice president of MySpace online marketing Sean Percival, "They looked at Friendster and said: 'Wow, people are spending insane amounts of time on this site. We should copy it.' And all they wanted to do was build a social network so they could have distribution for their ads, selling these horrible products to people. And that's where it began."[141] They pitched the idea of a different social site to their ex-bosses and MySpace was born in 2003.

Rather than using a social network, MySpace allowed a member to scan users at will. The immediate circle of friends model that Friendster had popularized was no longer a barrier to checking people out. Scanning opened new possibilities for dating and social connectivity, and the basic software performed better than previous networks. One could also customize one's own profile page to make it a truly personal space. And because the site initially targeted bands and actors in Los Angeles, MySpace had a certain coolness built in. If Friendster focused on friend networks, MySpace would quickly shift the focus of the social toward one of self-promotion and online sexual encounters. It provided a platform for self-expression.

The growth was historic. Between 2005 and 2006, the membership grew from 2 million to 80 million.[142] At its peak, MySpace would attract 100 million unique visitors a month. In 2005, MySpace found itself in the midst of a bidding war between Fox's Rupert Murdoch and Viacom. Fox got the deal and purchased MySpace and parent company Intermix Media for an insane $580 million. It was considered a great deal at the time (and would later be considered one of the largest mistakes in net history). With the purchase came pressure to spur ad revenue. Google signed up to be the sole search engine for MySpace by offering a price of $300 million a year for three years.[143] Part of that deal included a series of metrics site traffic would need to reach, and so advertisements doubled on the site.

As it would happen, the company founded by people who worked to clog the internet with ads would find their own site clogged with ads. In addition, the ability to freely move about profile pages led to users posing as other people, and MySpace, as dating sites tend to do, quickly became home to escalating spam and predatory behavior. Sexual paranoia became rampant, and as we know, fear of sex plays into the media's hands like wildfire (particularly when it is a rival media company, not only a platform). In 2009, MySpace announced that it had removed 90,000 registered sex offender members.[144] Was that supposed to be comforting?

MySpace soon became a megacompany obsessed with revenue—an attempt at a sort of social-media Amazon. They added features from video to blogs, from karaoke to book clubs. They tried everything and eventually the site became, as Sean Percival describes it, "a massive spaghetti-ball mess." After numerous staff shake-ups, including the canning of the founders, the site was sold in 2011 for $35 million. And while the sale of the company didn't necessarily reflect its social value (Indymedia, for example, never had a sale price), in this case, as a site whose birth was exclusively for capitalist purposes, the sales price perfectly reflected its social power. Percival notes, "There are companies that do not get social and they never will. Apple's one of them, Google is the other: they've failed with Google+. When your culture is engineering-focused, you do not understand social. Social is a very emotional experience. Engineers are not so much, in a lot of cases."[145]

How did these early social platforms transform social relationships? How did it affect our sense of romance? Our sense of sex? Our sense of time? How many hours in the day do kids spending scrolling through profiles? How many hours are spent taking pictures to post online? This massive shift in scale is the true revolution of social networks. They radically altered the ways in which the cultural world produced itself.

OF iPODS AND iPHONES

It takes a while for a string of code that interprets switches on a circuit board to find its way into the collective emotional fabric of a planet, but give it time, and it will. In Apple's 2003 ad campaign for iPod, and eventually iTunes—simply referred to as the Silhouette campaign—a silhouetted figure with an iconic white iPod (designed by Apple designer Jonathan Ives) and headphones rocks out to their music and the world around goes electric with color. It tempts the viewer with a seductive picture of computers' contemporary relationship to the world: the computer can bring the intimate into deep connection with the public. That is to say, the intimate world could come to entirely paint over the external. Like Apple's 1984 campaign, the pitch did, in at least one manner of speaking, match the reality. iPod, like iMac, would pull the external world into closer proximity to the self. And soon, the iPhone would revolutionize the planet.

A computer held in the hand, the iPhone made physically mobile the capabilities of some of the world's most powerful machines. Camera, messenger, calendar, e-mail, video games, weather, jogging, the sky was the limit for this pocket-friendly digital appendage. The introduction of the iPhone was not merely a technology, it became a powerful tool in resculpting the social sphere.

The origins of the iPhone stem back to Steve Jobs's interest in a touch-screen interface. He sought the finger-feeling that had only partially been achieved by the mouse. The iPhone released in 2007 did this and so much more.

The phone was, obviously, a gigantic financial success. Designed again by Ives, the iPhone made sensual this device that would soon become an integral part of the collective corporality. The world of computers was in your pocket, buzzing against your skin with humble urgency and nerve-ending attachment.

GETTING SOCIAL

At this point it is useful to turn more reflectively toward the social dimension of these technological innovations.

When Sean Percival glibly notes that some companies "get social," what does this mean? It is a simple insight that is the tip of the iceberg. For in "getting social," we see a certain respect for the Bernays sensibility that had been ripping through the personal computer and online world for the last twenty years. If Bernays believed that third-party experts could help one decide to choose a brand, the opinions of close friends could help one even more. The "like" button has come to define what it means to aggregate social approval and the behavior of the multitude by way of their complex social networks. Not only is social networking a massive part of contemporary urban life, it has also altered in a profound manner that thing called public opinion. If culture is a weapon, social networking is a mighty large weapon indeed.

After the demise of MySpace came the astronomical rise of Facebook. Its success has been attributed to everything from its invite-only beginnings, to a return to more immediate friend networks, to a more defined anti-advertising position for many of its initial years, to a more streamlined approach to the site's back end, to allowing outside firms to develop Facebook-friendly tools operating in a simpler source code. But whatever the case, the scale is unprecedented. In the first quarter of 2016, the site hit 1.65 billion active monthly users (there are 7.125 billion people on the planet). It has come to define the social sphere.

Certainly other sites have emerged as well. Twitter (315 million active users), LinkedIn (100 million active users), Instagram (200 million active users), YouTube, Pinterest,

Tumblr, Flickr, and Reddit (and once this is printed, these names will inevitably feel dated as new platforms and technologies will emerge). But like the early era of radio, and the early era of television, our dominant mode of cultural programming (social media) is in an early stage where the technological implications on the social are just now being felt.

In their book *Connected: How Your Friend's Friends' Friends Affect Everything You Feel, Think, and Do*, professors Nicholas A. Christakas, Ph.D., and James H. Fowler ask a basic question: what is a social network and how does it affect who we are? Part of the answer is that a social network is something that we had long taken for granted, but had never been truly visible until now. A person might have always been aware that they operated in a particular social milieu. We had friends who knew each other. We knew there were people we simply had no connection to: either because they were in a different class, a different culture, a different geography, a different religion, and on and on. We understood, intuitively, that social networks were part of our daily lives.

In their book, Christakas and Fowler demonstrate that we are shaped not only by the opinions of our friends, but even our friends' friends, and more than that, our friends' friends' friends. Taking that insight exponentially, one finds that a social network not only is important in understanding who we spend time with, but also in how we think.

Today, online social networks tap into something

deeply personal as they become a glue between our friendships and relationships. While some adults might find such information marginally hyperbolic, for many teens (those whose entire ontology are shaped by social-networking platforms) the truth of this connection is extremely evident. A report from Common Sense Media found that 75 percent of American teenagers were on social-networking sites, and that they have found themselves deeply enmeshed in an entirely new realm of mediated social relationships and affects.[146] From cyberbullying to sexting, the phenomena of the social network sets the terms of how today's teens engage with their world.

And, of course, not only teens are affected. The entire public realm has shifted. When you see people checking their phones, they are both here and not here. Before we take for granted the shift that has occurred in our social and intimate worlds, we must try to understand the degree to which this world emerged out of a history of proprietary ownership and sales. As we've learned, the weapon that is culture—and its constant appeal to the most intimate parts of our selves—is rarely used for purely benevolent purposes.

EMOTIONAL CONTAGIONS AS INFORMATION

Social networks have become powerful sites for the spread of information. Personal updates are seamlessly integrated with the forwarding of news articles, silly cat videos, and celebrity gossip. All information crosses the screen in a similar format, and is received in a similar manner. Traditional news outlets have felt the earth shake beneath them as advertising revenues have dropped, and the very methods by which we circulate news have changed drastically.

As Clay Shirky writes in his book, *Here Comes Everybody*, "The mass amateurization of publishing undoes the limitations inherent in having a small number of traditional press outlets."[147] Suddenly blogs, like the simple sharing features on most social-networking platforms, became a powerful vehicle for sharing news. As information became democratized so too did the tone and emotional space of that very information. Information, whether it was about a breakup or about a school crisis, became part of the affective space of intimate communication.

Christakas and Fowler articulate just how much our social networks affect what we think. They detail a story of what is clinically referred to as *massive psychogenic illness* (MPI), which is an outbreak of an emotional state. One can think of it as an emotional contagion, not unlike what stoners call a *contact high* (where one feels high simply from being around people who are high). "Experiments have demonstrated that people can 'catch' emotional states they observe in others over time frames ranging from seconds to weeks."[148] As social networks become the dominant manner in which news (even the word news needs redefining at this point) is experienced, the texture of that news changes. It becomes affective. And as we have seen detailed throughout this book, the range of human emotion is not value neutral. Certain emotions move information faster than others.

Any person who has spent a few years on the internet has become accustomed to a certain heightened emotional content, the anxious tone, of certain social-media tropes. It is sort of like watching the panic nature of Fox News twenty-four seven, even if the ideological content varies.

In November 2012, the satirical magazine the *Onion* posted a headline that read: "After Obama Victory, Shrieking White-Hot Sphere of Pure Rage Early GOP Front-Runner for 2016." Satirical but true. During the culture wars of the 1980s, indignation would fuel the Republican strategy, but such emotional appeals have come to dominate all forms of political content.

In their paper, "Emotions and Information Diffusion in Social Media—Sentiment of Microblogs and Sharing Behavior," Stefan Stielglits and Linh Dang-Xuan report the most obvious of findings: "Based on two data sets of more than 165,000 tweets in total, we find that emotionally charged Twitter messages tend to be retweeted more often and more quickly compared to neutral ones. As a practical implication, companies should pay more attention to the analysis of sentiment related to their brands and products in social-media communication as well as in designing advertising content that triggers emotions."[149] Nothing like scientists using their intelligent findings to tell companies how to take advantage of people's emotions.

An online-marketing blog specifically advises marketers to avoid the emotions of joy (because that media space is already clogged with marketers) and sadness, and instead focus the emotional packaging of their products in anger and surprise.[150] No wonder the emotional space of information feels supercharged in the era of social media.

If the election of Obama in 2008 didn't already point to a certain shift in the space of information (and earlier on Howard Dean), then the rise of Donald Trump should definitely provide a fascinating backdrop. A man whose very temperament seems nearly engineered in its high velocity of paranoia, conspiracy, and indignation, his highly tweetable phraseologies connect to a seething world of alienated bodies of America.

But rather than focusing on what Trump is saying (such a task might be nigh impossible), one has to appreciate the emotional texture of what is said, and how that texture— whether fear, racial paranoia, indignation, or surprise— plays into the virality of emotionally charged information. Trump is appealing not because of his brazen lack of political correctness, but because he is always surprising, angry, and sharing in your fears. And these emotions are deeply contagious. The individual, as studies point out, is sensitive to the feelings of the group, and social networks only reinforce this logic—at higher speeds and over greater distances than ever before. It was like this with the speeches of Hitler in the 1930s, it was like this during the culture wars of the 1980s, it was like this with televised images of the war on drugs of the 1990s.

One must step back to fully appreciate what makes our current moment so unique. One of the largest commercial markets is the cyberspace of social communication and interaction. The privatized space of the internet has monetized the basic functions of sociality. One of the foundational elements of what we consider culture (sociability) has become a central space of the global economy at a scale that is mind-boggling. Culture is a weapon, because culture is making the world turn around.

And yet, with that said, not even the likes of Mark Zuckerberg or Steve Jobs could have foreseen the kind of social transformations the advent of the computer and social networking have had. Just because something makes money doesn't mean you understand why or what else it is doing. Ultimately, the shift toward a self-production of media has transformed how we understand ourselves, and how we construct the political narratives that interpret the world of power around us.

REVOLUTION GOES VIRAL

The tech-media referred to the Arab Spring of 2011 as the Twitter Revolution, and while it is utterly off the mark to credit Twitter for the spread of protests that swept the Mideast, one has to appreciate the power that social media provided in disrupting the ruling regime's narrative of power. Like all revolutions, and particularly ones spread virally by way of social media, the actual event itself is more akin to a swarm than unilateral action. And that swarm managed to change the face of Egypt and beyond. With thousands of young people, and some older, occupying the central Tahrir Square, a face-off occurred with the governmental forces of President Hosni Mubarak.

Twelve years after the demonstrations against the WTO in Seattle and the initiation of the Indymedia, the revolutionary potential of the internet had moved from isolated computers to cell phones that many of the protestors carried. As opposed to a central site like Indymedia to post to, the information was spread through individual efforts across the city, country, and planet. Virality had already been demonstrated with cat videos and Kanye West tweets, but in 2011 it became clear that the vectors controlling public opinion were in flux.

The revolution in Egypt was not without its violence, with 846 people killed and over 6,000 injured. Clashes with the military came with brutal oppression. But like a swarm of ants, the people kept returning to the square in increasing numbers. Eventually, as we know, Mubarak would step down and a new, albeit complex, chapter in Egyptian history would begin.

In the aftermath, *Time* magazine had to find a face to put to the movement. They focused on Egyptian social-networking entrepreneur and Google's then Mideast marketing chief Wael Ghonim, naming him in *Time*'s "100 Most Influential People of 2011." Certainly Ghonim played a role, but like Occupy to come and #BLM after, the uses of culture by social media play more by the logic of the masses than that of the single-minded entrepreneur.

Ghonim had been one of two administrators on a Facebook page from 2010 "We are all Khaled Saeed." Khaled Saleed was a young man who was dragged from a cyber café in Alexandria by police and beat to death. Ghonim's Facebook page gained tremendous interest, and he was subsequently interrogated and detained for eleven days. After a televised interview, Ghonim became a sensation. In an interview with CNN, Ghonim states, "I want to meet Mark Zuckerburg one day and thank him actually," he said. "Tell him to call me."[151]

But the revolutions would only continue to spread. Beginning in Tunisia, moving to Egypt and then spreading to Libya, Yemen, and Syria, these protests would be called the Arab Spring. Then came the European Summer of Spain and Greece, and then the Occupy Movement in the Fall of 2011 starting in Zuccotti Park and spreading across the United States. By October 2011, 900 cites across the planet had hosted their own version of Occupy.

The virality of these movements is not only a testament to social media, but perhaps, more important, the manner in which social media facilitates and thus perpetuates already deeply felt desires in a broad public. If indignation is one of the internet's most poignant emotional attributes, the broad public has much to be indignant about. Autocratic puppet regimes in Egypt and Syria, neoliberal policies crushing the working class in Greece and Spain, and a rising 1 percent class in the United States, as well as a flagrantly racist and murderous policy toward African Americans. Indignation does not only have shock value on its side, but helps an avalanche of truth come to light. Said another way, videos of cops killing kids are not only affectively powerful images to circulate on the internet, they also, and more important, lay bare the conditions of power in everyday people's lives.

Certainly there are plenty of critics, not only of social media's prominence, but its ability to organize. In the United States the diverse and self-labeled Occupy Wall Street refused to have any specific demands, and #BLM refused to endorse any political candidates during the 2016 primary. More than a few pundits have stated that these movements lack proper teeth in making *real* political change. Unlike the Tea Party, the argument went, Occupy and Black Lives Matter were unsuccessful when it came to forcing their political positions into the halls of governance. But such critiques lack an appreciation for the shifting ground of culture, as well as an understanding of these movements as a barometer for political consciousness.

While birds of a feather might flock together in social media, they also appear to, over time, evolve the political discussion as well. During Twitter and Facebook's rapid ascent, *socialism* was no longer a bad word among young people. At the same time, flagrantly racist language and tabloid-esque behavior had become not only a norm for Trump, but also had become a clearly effective strategy. It appears that social media, for good and bad, became our most powerful tool for shaping the political range of debate in American elections.

CONCLUSION

In conclusion, I want to state something very obvious: the computer is a very powerful device. Steve Jobs had a vision of a tool that would appeal to the very emotional and intimate needs of the mass consumer market. With the help of the designer Ivy, he accomplished that. But the computer has also become an apparatus that augments the intimate needs of a person. More than just an image that expresses intimacy, the computer powerfully extends the reach of each person that uses one.

With the advent of the internet and social media, this extension has melded the public and private into a powerful fulcrum that will rival the printing press in its effects on the entire ontology (or public opinion) of the people of this earth.

We see its effects in small things already. The twitchy behavior of friends needing to check their phones. The inability to let a question linger too long before one looks it up on Google. The worry that everyone knows what you have been, and are, up to. The inability to get lost.

Human behaviors are changing. And while computers have greatly facilitated this shift, it would be a mistake to think the corporate boards and their ever-pernicious advertisers know where this is headed. Even equipped with extraordinary consumer analytics that knows if you like a book on the Zapatistas, for example, you might also like a book about the internet and the Iranian Revolution, the brains behind these megacompanies can only understand

the effect of these gears in the short term. For those hobbyists, dreamers, and anyone else who imagines the uses of
these technologies beyond that of just making money, the
horizon is quite broad and the possibilities incredible.

Certainly, like the corporate social spaces of IKEA,
Apple Store, and Starbucks, there is reasonable concern regarding the privatization of online social space. Facebook
is neither neutral nor democratic. It uses its power of collective culture as a weapon to garner revenue. And as much
as Google continues to espouse a brand of "Do No Evil,"
it continues to operate, like all businesses, with one goal
in mind: longstanding financial growth. And finally, as
much as Apple will enjoins us to "Think Different," their
longstanding commitment to proprietary software and
hardware, as well as a not-so-different model of off-shore
manufacturing, makes their story a little less romantic. Yes,
capitalism is alive and well in the supposedly revolutionary
era of Silicon Valley.

But that said—and that caveat is absolutely critical—the
computer is even more than a machine for capitalism. Like
the radio before, its galvanizing effects could lead us to
anything from horrific genocide to challenges to capitalism itself. It could help invent a new kind of rock and roll
or reinforce our worst fears about each other. Simply put,
it is the latest and most powerful tool in the ongoing technological endeavor to connect with and mobilize the oh-so
intimate part of each of us.

ACKNOWLEDGMENTS

I wrote this book in a post–Occupy Wall Street mood and after the completion of my first book, *Seeing Power*. I had just finished the exhibition Living as Form and was eager to have a companion volume of artistic practices that weren't necessarily doing "good" things in the world. You could think of it as the b-side of the well-intentioned socially engaged arts. In that spirit, I started the journey on this project and it has been an incredible and eye-opening ride. During that period so much has changed and my thoughts on so many things have evolved.

I want to thank my dear friends Trevor Paglen, Matt Littlejon, Aaron Gach, Daniel Tucker, Karyn Behnke, Collin Reno and Gregory Sholette, for their friendship. I want to thank my ever-evolving team at Creative Time (Katie, Jean, Sally, Cynthia, Alyssa, Marisa, Natasha, Alex, Teal, Ashley, Eric, Ella, Drew) and the board who have been such great people to work and dream with. I have to thank my editors at Melville House (Mark Krotov and Ryan Harrington) as well as Dennis and Valerie and the whole Melville House team.

I want to thank some people whose work has been of great influence on this book including Jeff Chang, Thomas Frank, Sue Bell Yank, Dan Wang, Rebecca Solnit, Tom Finklepearl, Shannon Jackson, Stephen Duncombe, Andrew Ross, again Gregory Sholette. I have to thank the artists and art people I have had the pleasure of working with and getting to know including Jonas Staahl, Ahmet Ogut, Sofia Hernandez Chong Cuy, Tania Bruguera, Paul Ramirez Jonas, Pablo Helguera, Jeremy Deller, J. Morgan Puett, Rashida Bumbrey, Elissa Blount Moorehead, Rylee Ertigrosso, Jennifer Scott, Rob Blackson, Ruth Blackson, Sheila Pree Bright, Mark Dion, Critical Art Ensemble, Future Farmers, Jon Rubin, Pedro Reyes, Duke Riley, Simone Leigh, Xenobia Bailey, Leroy Johnson, Theadore Harris, Theresa Rose, Abigail Satinksy, Anthony Romero, and Kara Walker. As abstract as it is, I have to thank the Occupy Wall Street folks that gave me so much to think about including Yates MacKee, Noah Fischer, Beka and Jason, Natasha, and Amin, the Gulf Labor folks, and the incredible movement shaping American history at this time, #BlackLivesMatter. I must certainly send big ups to my mother and father. And finally, I have to thank my incredible wife Theresa who has brought so much joy, and much needed feedback, into my life and our beautiful dreaming child, Elias.

NOTES

All websites accessed Setember 19, 2016, unless otherwise noted.

INTRODUCTION

1. "Advertisers Will Spend Nearly $600 Billion Worldwide in 2015," *eMarketer*, December 10, 2014, www.emarketer.com /Article/Advertisers-Will-Spend-Nearly-600-Billion-World-wide-2015/1011691.
2. Jeffrey Van Camp, "91 Percent of Kids Play Video Games, Study Says," *Digital Trends*, October 11, 2011, www.digitaltrends.com /computing/91-percent-of-kids-play-video-games-says-study/.
3. Jordan Shapiro, "Teenagers in the U.S. Spend About Nine Hours a Day in Front of a Screen," *Forbes*, November 3, 2015, www.forbes.com/sites/jordanshapiro/2015/11/03/teenagers-in-the-u-s-spend-about-nine-hours-a-day-in-front-of-a-screen/#3dd542f47c34.

CHAPTER I: THE REAL CULTURE WAR

4. Cynthia Koch, "The Contest for American Culture: A Leadership Case Study on The NEA and NEH Funding Crisis," *Public Talk* (1998), www.upenn.edu/pnc/ptkoch.html.
5. Dominick Dunne, "Robert Mapplethorpe's Proud Finale," *Van-*

ity Fair, September 5, 2013, www.vanityfair.com/culture/1989
/02/robert-mapplethorpe-aids-dominick-dunne.

6. www.chicagoreader.com/chicago/messages-to-dread
/Content?oid=874937.

7. Richard Bolton, *Culture Wars: Documents from the Recent Controversies in the Arts* (New York: New Press, 1992), 210.

8. Steven C. Dubin, *Arresting Images: Impolitic Art and Uncivil Actions* (New York: Routledge, 1994), 156.

9. Ibid.

10. Bolton, 210.

11. Ibid.

12. Sara Rimer, "Obscenity or Art? Trial on Rap Lyrics Opens," *The New York Times*, October 17, 1990, www.nytimes.com/1990
/10/17/us/obscenity-or-art-trial-on-rap-lyrics-opens.html.

13. "Number of TV Households in America," *Television History—the First 75 Years*, www.tvhistory.tv/Annual_TV_Households_50-78.jpg.

CHAPTER 2: THE PERSUADERS

14. lamar.colostate.edu/~pr/ivylee.pdf, p. 268.

15. en.wikipedia.org/wiki/Ludlow_Massacre.

16. Brendan Bruce, "On the Origins of Spin (or How Hollywood, the Ad Men and the World Wide Web Became the Fifth Estate and Created Our Images of Power)," CreateSpace Independent Publishing Platform, June 2013, p. 19.

17. en.wikipedia.org/wiki/Espionage_Act_of_1917.

18. Oren Stephens, *Facts to a Candid World: America's Overseas Information Program* (Palo Alto: Stanford University Press, 1955), 32.

19. Ronald Steel, *Walter Lippmann and the American Century* (Herndon, VA: Transaction Publishers, 1980), 125.

20. Stuart Ewan, *PR!: A Social History of Spin* (New York: Basic Books, 1996), 127.

21. Jennifer S. Lee, "Big Tobacco's Spin on Women's Liberation," City Room (blog), *The New York Times*, October 10, 2008, city-room.blogs.nytimes.com/2008/10/10/big-tobaccos-spin-on-womens-liberation/?_r=0.

22. Larry Tye, *The Father of Spin: Edward L. Bernays and the Birth of Public Relations* (New York: Picador, 2002), 30.

23. Edward Bernays, *Crystallizing Public Opinion* (New York: Ig Publishing, 2011), 129.

24. Ibid., 25.

25. Edward Bernays, *Propaganda* (New York: Ig Publishing), 73.

26. B. Z. Doktorov, *George Gallup: Biography and Destiny* (Moscow: Polygraph Inform, 1990), romir.ru/GGallup_en.pdf, 74.

27. Ibid., 75.

28. Ibid.

29. Mansel Blackford and K. Austin Kerr, "The Rise of Marketing and Advertising," in *Business Enterprise in American History* (Boston: Cengage Learning, 1993), faculty.atu.edu/cbrucker/Engl5383/Marketing.htm.

30. Stephen Fox, *Mirror Makers: A History of American Advertising and Its Creators* (Urbana-Champagn: University of Illinios Press, 1997), 81.

31. Susan E. Gallagher, "TIMELINE: History of Radio & Politics," faculty.uml.edu/sgallagher/radiotimeline.htm.

32. Joseph Goebbels, "Der Rundfunk als achte Großmacht," *Signale der neuen Zeit. 25 ausgewählte Reden von Dr. Joseph Goebbels* (Munich: Zentralverlag der NSDAP, 1938), research.calvin.edu/german-propaganda-archive/goeb56.htm.

33. Randall Bytwerk, "First Course for Gau and County," en.wikipedia.org/wiki/Nazi_propaganda (retrieved June 19, 2014).

CHAPTER 3: THE PERSUADERS, PART II

34. Horkheimer, M., and Adorno, T. W. (1972). *Dialectic of enlightenment.* New York, Herder and Herder, p. 39.

35. Thomas Gate, "The American Film Industry in the Early 1950s," Encyclopedia.com, www.encyclopedia.com/article-1G2-2584300013/american-film-industry-early.html.

36. Christina Harold, *OurSpace: Resisting the Corporate Control of Culture* (Minneapolis: University of Minnesota Press, 1999), books.google.com/books?id=klhvzgjT2QkC&pg=PA4&lpg=PA4&dq=situationists+and+charlie+chaplin&source=bl&ots=B8SIYhONj5&sig=SkqaFLAVR5RXcVKyWzsJKjSUIE8&hl=en&sa=X&ei=EtoJVI-ol5OjyASbvoCwDQ&ved=0CE4Q6AEwCw#v=onepage&q=situationists%20and%20charlie%20chaplin&f=false.

37. Bernard Bailyn et al., *The Great Republic: A History of the American People* (Lexington, Mass.: D.C. Heath, 1985), 794.

38. pmc.iath.virginia.edu/text-only/issue.104/14.2banash.txt, quoted in Lotringer, 262.

39. pmc.iath.virginia.edu/text-only/issue.104/14.2banash.txt.

40. Mark Tungate, *Adland: A Global History of Marketing* (London: Kogan Page, 2013), 68.

CHAPTER 4: FEAR MACHINES

41. Thomas Frank, *The Conquest of Cool: Business Culture, Counterculture, and the Rise of Hip Consumerism* (Chicago: University of Chicago Press, 1997), 6.

42. Timothy Patrick McCarthy and John McMillian, *Protest Nation: Words That Inspired a Century of American Radicalism* (New York: New Press, 2010), 175.

43. Edward Bernays, *Crystalizing Public Opinion* (New York: Ig Publishing, 2011), 164.

44. This quote comes from an interview conducted by Alexander Lamis, a professor of political science at Case Western University. The quote first appeared in his 1984 book *The Two-Party South* without attribution. Eight years after Atwater's death, Lamis revealed his source in another book.

45. *The New Jim Crow: Mass Incarceration in the Age of Colorblindness* by Michelle Alexander, New Press, New York, 2013, p. 49.

46. Ibid.

47. www.themarshallproject.org/2015/05/01/a-more-or-less-definitive-guide-to-hillary-clinton-s-record-on-law-and-order#.j3mErVvzR.

48. Brigitte L. Nacos, Yaeli Bloch-Elkon, and Robert Y. Shapiro, *Selling Far: Counterterrorism, the Media and Public Opinion* (Chicago: University of Chicago Press, 2011), 29.

49. Ibid., 35.

50. Ibid., xxxvi.

51. Giorgio Agamben, *Homo Sacer: Sovereign Power and Bare Life*, trans. D. Heller-Roazen (Palo Alto: Stanford University Press, 1998), 168.

52. Stephen Duncombe, *Dream: Re-imagining Progress in an Age of Fantasy* (New York: New Press, 2007), 124.

53. Ibid., 174.

CHAPTER 5: THE REAL ESTATE SHOW

54. Richard Florida, *Rise of the Creative Class*, rev. ed. (New York: Basic Books, 2012), vii.

55. ceosforcities.org/wp-content/uploads/2015/12/Branding-Your-City.pdf.

56. "Holy Cow!: Businessman Peter Hanig Had a Dream to Make Chicago Go Bullish on Bovines," *People*, August 30, 1999, www.people.com/people/archive/article/0,,20129084,00.html.

57. David Ng, "NEA's Rocco Landesman: No More Culture Wars," Culture Monster (blog), *Los Angeles Times*, October 21, 2009, latimesblogs.latimes.com/culturemonster/2009/10/neas-rocco-landesman-downplays-partisan-fighting-emphasizes-optimism.html.

58. Vitality Index 2011, Creative Cities International LLC, creativecities.org/wp-content/uploads/2012/04/VI-exec-summary-071811.pdf.

59. Brendan Colgan, "Creative Cities International—The Vitality Index (VI)," *Places: A Critical Geography Blog*, blog.inpolis.com/2011/12/07/creative-cities-international-the-vitality-index-vi.

60. Richard Florida, "Gentrification," Creative Class, www.creativeclass.com/_v3/creative_class/2008/01/08/gentrification/.

61. Richard Lloyd, *Neo-Bohemia: Art and Commerce in the PostIndustrial City* (New York: Routledge, 2006), 239.

62. Rosalind Deutsche, *Evictions: Art and Spatial Politics* (Cambridge: MIT Press, 1996), 151.

63. "The Real Estate Show," 98Bowery: 1969–89, 98bowery.com/returntothebowery/abcnorio-the-real-estate-show.php.

64. Ibid.

65. Jillian Steinhauer, "The Real Story Behind the Gentrification of Brooklyn," *Hyperallergic*, February 1, 2013, hyperallergic.com/64500/the-real-story-behind-the-gentrification-of-brooklyn/.

CHAPTER 6: THE INSURGENTS

66. Dexter Filkins, "844 in U.S. Military Killed in Iraq in 2005," *The New York Times*, January 1, 2006, www.nytimes.com/2006/01/01/international/middleeast/01iraq.html?_r=0.

67. U.S. Department of the Army, *Counterinsurgencies*, Field Manual

3-24 (Washington, D.C.: U.S. Department of the Army, December 2006), usacac.army.mil/cac2/Repository/Materials/COIN-FM3-24.pdf.

68. Ibid.

69. Rochelle Davis, "Culture as Weapon," *Middle East Research and Information Project* 40 (Spring 2010), www.merip.org/mer/mer255/culture-weapon.

70. Gareth Porter, "How Petraeus Created the Myth of His Success," *Truthout*, November 27, 2012, truth-out.org/news/item/12997-how-petraeus-created-the-myth-of-his-success.

71. Michael R. Gordon, "The Struggle for Iraq Reconstruction: 101st Airborne Scores Success in Northern Iraq, *The New York Times*, September 4, 2003.

72. Joe Klein, "Good General, Bad Mission," *Time*, January 12, 2007, www.time.com/time/nation/article/0,8599,1587186,00.html.

73. Michael R. Gordon, "The Struggle for Iraq: Reconstruction; 101st Airborne Scores Success in Northern Iraq," *The New York Times*, September 4, 2013, www.nytimes.com/2003/09/04/international/worldspecial/04NORT.html.

74. Fred Kaplan, *The Insurgents: David Petraeus and the Plot to Change the American Way of War* (New York: Simon & Schuster, 2013), 28.

75. Benjamin C. Schwarz, *American Counterinsurgency Doctrine and El Salvador: The Frustrations of Reform and the Illusions of Nation Building* (Santa Monica, CA: RAND Corporation, 1991), www.rand.org/content/dam/rand/pubs/reports/2006/R4042.pdf.

76. U.S. Department of the Army, *Counterinsurgencies*, Field Manual 3-24.

77. Kaplan, 266.

78. Adam Curtis has shadowed the writing of this book as he not only shares an interest in Bernays but also in COIN. Through his films, essays, and blogs, perhaps more than any other contemporary figure, he has avidly pursued an investigation of the ramifications of a world of powerful actors cynically operating with a knowledge of culture.

79. Adam Curtis, "How to Kill a Rational Peasant," *The Medium and the Message* (blog), BBC.co.uk, June 16, 2012, www.bbc.co.uk/blogs/adamcurtis/posts/how_to_kill_a_rational_peasant.

80. David Galula, "From Algeria to Iraq: All But Forgotten Les-

sons from Nearly 50 Years Ago," *RAND Review* 30, no. 2 (Summer 2006), www.rand.org/pubs/periodicals/rand-review /issues/summer2006/algeria.html.

81. Saul Alinsky, *Rules for Radicals: A Pragmatic Primer for Realistic Radicals* (New York: Random House, 2010), 127–30.

82. humanterrainsystem.army.mil/about.html.

83. "American Anthropological Association's Executive Board Statement on the Human Terrain System Project," American Anthropological Association, November 6, 2007, www.foothill.edu/attach/AAA_statement_human_terrain.pdf.

84. Montgomery McFate and Andrea Jackson, "*An Organizational Solution to DOD's Cultural Knowledge Needs,*" *Military Review* (July–August 2005), 18–21, www.au.af.mil/au/awc/awcgate/milre view/mcfate2.pdf.

85. Montgomery McFate, "Anthropology and Counterinsurgency: The Strange Story of Their Curious Relationship," *Military Review* (March–April 2005): 24–38.

86. Matthew B. Stannard, "Montgomery McFate's Mission: Can One Anthropologist Possibly Steer the Course in Iraq?" sfgate .com, April 29, 2007, www.sfgate.com/magazine/article/Montgomery-McFate-s-Mission-Can-one-2562681.php#page-1.

87. Allan Kaprow and Jeff Kelley, *Essays on the Blurring of Art and Life*, ed. Jeff Kelley (Berkeley: University of California Press, 1993), 62.

88. Noah Shachtman, "'Human Terrain' Chief Ousted," *Wired*, June 15, 2010, www.wired.com/dangerroom/2010/06/human-terrain-chief-ousted/.

89. Robert Young Pelton, "Afghanistan: The New War for Hearts and Minds," *Men's Journal* (February 2009), www.mensjournal.com/magazine/afghanistan-the-new-war-for-hearts-and-minds-20130625?page=1.

90. iluvamaninuniform.blogspot.com/.

CHAPTER 7: SOUNDING THE TRUMPET

91. "Campbell's History Intro," The Digital Deli Online, www .digitaldeliftp.com/LookAround/advertspot_campbells.htm.

92. "Campbell Soup Co.," AvertisingAge, September 15, 2003, adage.com/article/adage-encyclopedia/campbell-soup/98376/.

93. "Campbell's Soup Can Changes Colors for Breast Cancer Awareness Month," BreastCancer.org, September 19, 2007, www.breastcancer.org/about_us/press_room/press_releases/2007/campbells_soup_changes_colors.

94. Stephanie Thompson, "Breast Cancer Awareness Strategy Increases Sales of Campbell's Soup," AdvertisingAge, October 3, 2006, adage.com/article/news/breast-cancer-awareness-strategy-increases-sales-campbell-s-soup/112198/.

95. Ibid.

96. "Soil Kitchen," Futurefarmers, www.futurefarmers.com/soil-kitchen/about.html.

97. Marcel Mauss, *The Gift: Forms and Functions of Exchange in Archaic Societies, Visions of Culture: An Introduction to Anthropological Theories and Theorists*, ed. Jerry D. Moore (Lanham, MD: Altamira Press, 2009), 127.

98. Robert H. Bremer, *Giving: Charity and Philanthropy in History* (Herndon, VA: Transaction Publishers, 1996), 39.

99. Peter Buffet, "The Charitable-Industrial Complex," *The New York Times*, July 26, 2013, www.nytimes.com/2013/07/27/opinion/the-charitable-industrial-complex.html?_r=0.

100. Ibid.

101. Brice S. McKeever, "The Nonprofit Sector in Brief 2015: Public Charities, Giving, and Volunteering," Urban Institute, Center on Nonprofits and Philanthropy, October 2015, www.urban.org/sites/default/files/alfresco/publication-pdfs/2000497-The-Nonprofit-Sector-in-Brief-2015-Public-Charities-Giving-and-Volunteering.pdf.

102. Hamish Pringle and Marjorie Thompson, *Brand Spirit: How Cause Related Marketing Builds Brands* (New York: Wiley, 2011), 3.

103. "Cause-Related Marketing," Knowledge Base, Grantspace, grantspace.org/tools/knowledge-base/Funding-Resources/Corporations/cause-related-marketing.

104. Pringle and Thompson, 5.

105. Ibid., 46.

106. Ted Purvis, *What We Want Is Free: Generosity and Exchange in Recent Art* (Albany: State University of New York Press, 2005).

CHAPTER 8: CORPORATE SOCIABILITY

107. Early Childhood Education and Care Policy in Sweden, OECD Country Note, December 1999, www.oecd.org/edu/school /2534972.pdf.

108. Ibid.

109. Ryan Gorman, "IKEA uses a staggering 1% of the world's wood every year," *Daily Mail*, July 5, 2013, www.dailymail.co.uk/news/article-2357216/IKEA-uses-staggering-1-worlds-wood-year.html.

110. inter.ikea.com/en/about-us/milestones/.

111. Adam Morgan, *Eating the Brand Fish: How Challenger Brands Can Compete Against Leading Brands* (New York: Wiley, 2009), 49.

112. Robert W. Wood, "Patriotic? After 40 Years Wandering in Tax Havens, IKEA Comes Home," *Forbes*, July 3, 2013, www .forbes.com/sites/robertwood/2013/07/03/patriotic-after-40-years-wandering-in-tax-havens-ikea-comes-home/.

113. "Ikea, eBay Avoid Paying UK Taxes, Reports Allege," *Huffington Post*, October 22, 2012, www.huffingtonpost.com/2012/10/22 /ikea-ebay-uk-taxes_n_2002016.html.

114. Michelle Higgins, "A Cheap Date with Child Care, by Ikea," *The New York Times*, June 10, 2009, www.nytimes.com/2009 /06/11/garden/11ikea.html.

115. "'The Hell of American Day Care': Expensive and 'Mediocre,'" NPR, www.npr.org/2013/04/17/177597801/the-hell-of-american-day-care-expensive-and-mediocre.

116. James Miller, "The Start of Something Big," *The New York Times*, February 20, 2000, www.nytimes.com/books/00/02 /20/reviews/000220.20millert.html.

117. Michael I. Norton, Daniel Mochon, and Dan Ariely, "The IKEA Effect: When Labor Leads to Love," *Journal of Consumer Psychology* 22 (3), 2012: 453–60.

118. "Ron Johnson: How I Built the Apply Store on Experience, Not Commissions," 9to5, November 21, 2011, 9to5mac.com /2011/11/21/ron-johnson-how-i-built-the-apple-store-on-experience-not-commisions/.

119. Sam Biddle, "How to Be a Genius: This Is Apple's Secret Training Manual," *Gizmodo*, August 28, 2012, gizmodo.com/5938323 /how-to-be-a-genius-this-is-apples-secret-employee-training-manual.

120. Jerry Useem, "How Apple Became the Best Retailer in the World," *Fortune*, March 8, 2007.

121. "Starbucks Company Statistics," *Statistic Brain*, September 6, 2016, www.statisticbrain.com/starbucks-company-statistics/.

122. "A Brief History of Coffee," *La Vita Dolce*, September 28, 2016, www.lavitadolcecafe.com/a-brief-history-of-coffee/.

123. Allan Kaprow, *Essays on the Blurring of Art and Life*, ed. Jeff Kelley (Berkeley: University of California Press, 1993), 59.

124. B. Joseph Pine II and James H. Gilmore, *The Experience Economy: Work Is Theater and Every Business a Stage* (Cambridge, MA: Harvard Business School Press, 1999), 2.

CHAPTER 9: THE EVER-SO-*PERSONAL* COMPUTER

125. "Internet Users," Internet Live Stats, www.internetlivestats.com/internet-users/.

126. Colin Campbell, "Here's How Many People Are Playing Games in America," *Polygon*, April 14, 2015, www.polygon.com/2015/4/14/8415611/gaming-stats-2015.

127. "Social Networking Reaches Nearly One in Four Around the World," eMarketer, June 18, 2013, www.emarketer.com/Article/Social-Networking-Reaches-Nearly-One-Four-Around-World/1009976.

128. Zach Epstein, "Horrifying Chart Reveals How Much Time We Spend Staring at Screens Each Day," BGR, May 29, 2014, bgr.com/2014/05/29/smartphone-computer-usage-study-chart/.

129. Advanced Research Projects Agency, April 23, 1963, www.chick.net/wizards/memo.html.

130. Bryan M. Leiner et al., "Brief History of the Internet," Internet Society, www.internetsociety.org/internet/what-internet/history-internet/brief-history-internet.

131. Sherry Turkle, *Alone Together: Why We Expect More from Technology and Less from Each Other* (New York: Basic Books, 2012), 157.

132. "EZLN's Declaration of War," flag.blackened.net/revolt/mexico/ezln/ezlnwa.html.

133. Ibid.

134. David Ronfeld, John Arquilla, Graham Fuller, and Melissa Fuller, *The Zapatista "Social Netwar" in Mexica* (Santa Monica, CA: RAND Corporation, 1998), 117.

135. Ibid., 4.

136. www.census.gov/prod/2001pubs/p23-207.pdf.

137. Brian McCullough, "A History of Internet Porn," History of Internet Podcast, January 4, 2015, www.internethistorypodcast.com/2015/01/history-of-internet-porn/.

138. thedinfographics.com/2011/12/23/internet-pornography-statistics/.

139. Brett Stalbaum, "The Zaptista Tactical Flood Net," www.thing.net/~rdom/ecd/ZapTact.html.

140. Max Chafkin, "How to Kill a Great Idea!," Inc.com, June 1, 2007, www.inc.com/magazine/20070601/features-how-to-kill-a-great-idea.html.

141. Stuart Dredge, "MySpace—What Went Wrong: 'The Site Was a Massive Spaghetti-Ball Mess,'" *The Guardian*, March 6, 2015, www.theguardian.com/technology/2015/mar/06/myspace-what-went-wrong-sean-percival-spotify.

142. "'A Place for Friends': A History of MySpace," RandomHistory.com, www.randomhistory.com/2008/08/14_myspace.html.

143. Felix Gillete, "The Rise and Inglorious Fall of Myspace," *Bloomberg*, June 22, 2011, www.bloomberg.com/news/articles/2011-06-22/the-rise-and-inglorious-fall-of-myspace.

144. Marion A. Walker, "My Space Removes 90,000 Sex Offenders," NBCnews.com, February 3, 2009, www.nbcnews.com/id/28999365/ns/technology_and_science-security/t/myspace-removes-sex-offenders/#.Vy5Q3BGCzww.

145. Dredge, "MySpace—What Went Wrong."

146. Suren Ramasubbu, "Influence of Social Media on Teenagers," *The Huffington Post*, May 26, 2015, www.huffingtonpost.com/suren-ramasubbu/influence-of-social-media-on-teenagers_b_7427740.html.

147. Clay Shirky, *Here Comes Everybody: The Power of Organizing Without Organization* (New York: Penguin Books, 2009), 65.

148. Christakas and Fowler, 35.

149. Stefan Stielglits and Linh Dang-Xuan, "Emotions and Information Diffusion in Social Media—Sentiment of Microblogs and Sharing Behavior," *Journal of Management Information Systems* 29(4):217–48, April 2013.

150. Matt Clough, "2 Emotions to Exploit (And 2 to Avoid) for Contagious Social Media Marketing," JeffBullas.com, www .jeffbullas.com/2015/11/18/2-emotions-exploit-2-avoid-conta-gious-social-media-marketing/.

151. Sajid Farooq, "Organizer of 'Revolution 2.0' Wants to Meet Mark Zuckerberg," *Press Here* (blog), NBC Bay Area, May 5, 2011, www.nbcbayarea.com/blogs/press-here/Egypts-Revolu-tion-20-Organizer-Wants-to-Thank-Mark-Zucker-berg-115924344.html.

ABOUT THE AUTHOR

NATO THOMPSON is Artistic Director at Creative Time, one of New York's most prestigious and exciting arts organizations. He is the editor of *Experimental Geography: Radical Approaches to Landscape, Cartography, and Urbanism* (Melville House); *The Interventionists: Users' Manual for the Creative Disruption of Everyday Life*; and *Living as Form: Socially Engaged Art from 1991–2011*. His most recent book is *Seeing Power: Art and Activism in the Twenty-first Century* (Melville House).